Mathematics in P

CONTEMPORARY ANALYSIS IN EDUCATION SERIES
General Editor: Philip Taylor

6 *Education and Cultural Pluralism*
  Edited by Maurice Craft

7 *Language and Learning: An Interactional Perspective*
  Edited by Gordon Wells and John Nicholls

8 *Educational Research: Principles, Policies and Practices*
  Edited by Marten Shipman

9 *Schooling and Welfare*
  Edited by Peter Ribbins

10 *Assessing Educational Achievement*
  Edited by Desmond L. Nuttall

11 *Education, Recession and the World Village*
  Edited by Frederick M. Wirt and Grant Harman

12 *Social Education: Principles and Practice*
  Edited by Chris Brown, Clive Harber and Janet Strivens

13 *Education and Society Today*
  Edited by Anthony Hartnett and Michael Naish

14 *Education and Youth*
  Edited by David Marsland

15 *Economics and the management of education: Emerging Themes*
  Edited by Hywel Thomas and Tim Simkins

16 *The Changing Primary School*
  Edited by Roy Lowe

17 *Mathematics in Primary Education*
  Edited by Michael Preston

Contemporary Analysis in Education Series

Mathematics in Primary Education

Edited by
MICHAEL PRESTON

 The Falmer Press

(A member of the Taylor & Francis Group)
London New York and Philadelphia

UK	The Falmer Press, Falmer House, Barcombe, Lewes, East Sussex, BN8 5DL
USA	The Falmer Press, Taylor & Francis Inc., 242 Cherry Street, Philadelphia, PA 19106–1906

© Selection and editorial material copyright M. Preston 1987

All rights reserved. No part of this publication may be reproduced, stored in a retrieval system, or transmitted in any form or by any means, electronic, mechanical, photocopying, recording or otherwise, without permission in writing from the Publisher.

First published 1987

Library of Congress Cataloging-in-Publication Data

Mathematics in primary education.

(Contemporary analysis in education series ; 17)
Includes index.
1. Mathematics—Study and teaching (Primary)—
Great Britain.   I. Preston, Michael.   II. Series.
QA135.5.M3693   1987   372.7'0941   87–15594
ISBN 1-85000-196-0
ISBN 1-85000-197-9 (pbk.)

Jacket design by Leonard Williams

Typeset in 11/13 Garamond by
Imago Publishing Ltd, Thame, Oxon

*Printed and bound in Great Britain by
Redwood Burn Limited, Trowbridge, Wiltshire*

Contents

General Editor's Preface Philip Taylor	vi
Introduction Michael Preston	vii
Planning the Curriculum Michael Preston	1
Teaching and Learning Mathematics in the Primary School David Owen	17
The Language of Primary Mathematics Janet Duffin	42
Mathematics Across the Curriculum Alan Sutcliffe	56
'Is It An Add, Miss?': Mathematics in the Early Primary Years Toni McPherson and Gill Payne	72
Mathematics in the Junior Years Christ Bailey	89
Calculators and Computers Brian Hughes	105
Mathematical Resources in the Primary School Jeffrey Goodwin	122
The Mathematics Adviser and Teacher Support Richard Strong	135
Assessment and Evaluation Peter Whitfield	151
Notes on Contributors	169
Index	171

General Editor's Preface

With the Cockcroft Report, *Mathematics Counts*, some five years old, it is time to take stock of where mathematics in primary education is at, where developments are most needed, what issues raised in the Report remain unresolved and what is happening at the frontiers of innovation. Taking stock is what this book does, and more. It provokes, prods and provides many practical examples of good teaching.

All the contributors are deeply involved in mathematics education as teachers, advisers, inspectors or in teacher education and each brings to their writing an eye for the practical concerns of teachers. It is this last which will make this collection of articles very successfully edited by Mike Preston of great value in the school and the college, for stimulus, insight and understanding as well as for reference.

But this collection does more than take stock and stimulate. It demonstrates that mathematics education in the primary school is not only important for the young in the modern world, it is also a more complex enterprise than many had thought. It does not provide any final answers, but it does, in its very accessibility, suggest that primary mathematics education is in an optimistic, hopeful state, with problems, yes, but also with solutions.

Philip Taylor
Birmingham June 1987

Introduction

It would be a brave person who could confidently predict the way forward in primary mathematics. Let it be clear from the outset that the intention of this volume is to provoke thought, discussion and identify possible developments. It is not to direct or indeed to suggest one particular way forward. Major reports have an impact but their effects are not necessarily long lasting. Thus it is not always easy to see in schools direct results from the Bullock Report. I suspect the same will be true of the Cockcroft Report. Indeed Hilary Shuard, President of the Mathematics Association, in her presidential address remarked that already some of the recommendations in the Cockcroft Report have become dated.

As editor, my invitation to contributors contained a wish that in the area of their particular specialism they considered approaches and identified issues to which the schools need to pay attention. The reader will not find therefore a common agreement or a well-developed argument running through the volume. Overall the book will provide a challenging appraisal of primary mathematics education. Individually each chapter contributes a dimension to the total weft and warp of mathematics education. Thus the reader whether headteacher, classroom teacher, student or educationist will be brought to an awareness of the complexity of factors involved in mathematics education.

As each piece is fitted together it becomes increasingly obvious that our national concern over achievement in mathematics must relate to the intricacy of the interrelated parts. For example, the crucial role that language plays in the child's early mathematical experience is highlighted by Janet Duffin and it takes considerable thought and experience to come to a full appreciation of the contribution that language can and should play. No sooner has this

Michael Preston

message been absorbed than other chapters jostle for attention in equally important areas, such as teaching style and approach or resources. Yet these examples do not relate to the changing face of mathematical content. The contribution on calculators and computers will challenge many readers to give careful thought to their own skills in these fields let alone consider the application to the primary classroom. The way forward can only lie in improved mathematical education at all stages. This means attention being given not only to the primary and secondary curriculum but to ensuring effective initial training and a regular programme of in-service teacher education.

It is hoped that this volume will contribute to our knowledge and thinking about primary mathematics education so that we can face the future with greater awareness.

Michael Preston
June 1987

Planning the Curriculum

Michael Preston

There has been more concern expressed over the general level of attainment reached in mathematics by pupils at the end of their full time education than in any other subject. Numerous DES and HMI publications reflect the worry over the real or apparent lack of mathematical knowledge and its application. Indeed, a major national enquiry into mathematical education begun in 1978 under the chairmanship of Dr WH Cockcroft[1] and published in 1982 identified specific weaknesses in the teaching and learning of mathematics. Three years later the Inspectorate published a consultative document *Mathematics from 5 to 16*[2] in the Curriculum Matters series. In the light of these and other publications since Curriculum Bulletin No 1: *Mathematics in the Primary School* in 1960,[3] where is mathematical education now?

I cannot approach the topic of planning the curriculum in mathematics with any degree of enthusiasm if it is to lead to yet another review of weaknesses, pious objectives for the future and exhortations to all to do better. Too many before me have trodden that path and in all honesty I do not see why I should be any more successful than they were. Nevertheless, before embarking on a consideration of the way forward an examination of some of the major weaknesses which it is alleged underlie the mathematics curriculum might suggest some fresh approach.

A good starting point for answering this question, and an encouraging one, is *Primary Education in England — A Survey by HM Inspectors of Schools*[4]. Here can be found in paragraphs 5.50 to 5.65 a fair appraisal of what was going on and a recognition that much of the basic content was appropriate and well matched to the child. However, the observations of HMI can be drawn together and two broad issues for consideration emerge. The first relates to teaching method and suggests that when dealing with the core or basic mathematical content, the teaching reflects competence but when an extension of this material is required, or when the application of the concepts arising from it to the broader framework of the curriculum is needed, then teaching is less effective. The second general observation seems to suggest that there is a lack of appreciation by teachers of progression in mathematical content so that the more able children are not challenged to develop their mathematical abilities and knowledge effectively.

The Cockcroft Report commences its chapter on Mathematics in the Primary years in an encouraging way:

> We have received much evidence which is supportive of the work of primary schools and believe that the great majority of primary teachers are aware of their responsibility to provide a sound mathematical foundation for the children in their care.

However, a closer look at this chapter needs to be undertaken to establish whether being aware of their responsibility is taken to the stage of teachers being able to carry out that responsibility. The Report draws attention to a number of recommendations and emphasizes some significant areas where it believes that the mathematical foundation laid in the primary school could be, and should be enhanced. Early on reference is made to the need for the mathematics curriculum to enrich children's aesthetic and linguistic experience.

> Language plays an essential part in the formulation and expression of mathematical ideas.[6]

This is a crucial dimension of mathematical education which is dealt with in a later chapter in this book. Immediately following this observation the Report stresses the importance of practical work and the need to practice mathematical skills in other areas of curricular experience.

In general terms, the Cockcroft Report seems to suggest broad agreement with the Primary Survey in that core material is reasonably well founded but that the primary mathematics curriculum, as it is taught in schools, lacks depth and application.

Advice for the future is contained in *Mathematics from 5 to 16*. In this publication Her Majesty's Inspectorate set out the expectations of mathematical education. In the early paragraphs (1.1 to

Planning the Curriculum

1.11) the sub-headings give an indication of the scope and range of what it is hoped schools will achieve:

Mathematics as an essential element of communication.
Mathematics as a powerful tool.
Appreciation of relationships within mathematics.
Awareness of the fascination of mathematics.
Imagination, initiative and flexibility of mind in mathematics.
Working in a systematic way.
Working independently.
Working cooperatively.
In-depth study of mathematics.
Pupils' confidence in their mathematical ability.[7]

These aims are far reaching and must provoke considerable thought to anyone concerned with planning a mathematics curriculum. The skills, knowledge and appreciation needed in order to perform satisfactorily over the ten broad aims listed above are considerable. Moreover these aims provide an immediate clue as to why there may be dissatisfaction with the current level of mathematics in primary schools. It is clear, and with no disrespect to primary teachers, I believe that a highly knowledgeable mathematics teacher with outstanding pedagogical skills would be required if these aims were to be satisfactorily achieved at the primary stage. Such teachers are few and rarely found in primary schools. Any curriculum planning must recognize this limitation. If some success is to be met over the full range of aims, then the curriculum process adopted must be capable of accommodating the teaching of mathematics to young children by skilled teachers who do not have the depth of mathematical knowledge and appreciation neccessary to achieve them across the full range of children's abilities.

Following a further exploration of the aims of teaching mathematics, HMI continue with the development of criteria that should underpin the development of curriculum content. However, it is clear that when teachers who are not specialist mathematicians try to come to grips with the criteria the enormity of the task will inevitably cause lack of confidence and a reaction that will lead to teaching 'that which we know and understand'.

This criticism does not lie with the intention, after all there would be few who would not agree with:

3

Mathematical content should form a coherent structure. Mathematical content should be sufficiently broad for all pupils. Mathematical content should include elements which are intrinsically interesting and important.[8]

These are but three examples from ten curriculum criteria. The problem lies in the translation of these generalized statements into specific content which will satisfy them.

The curriculum criteria are followed by the principles which need to underlie classroom approaches to mathematical teaching. Here again little criticism can be levelled against the intention or the range of teaching skills and method suggested:

A firm conceptual basis.
Flexibility.
Exposition by the teacher.
Problem solving.[9]

These are but four of the twelve principles to guide teaching. It now becomes necessary for the curriculum planning exercise to take note of ten aims leading to ten criteria for the selection of content and twelve principles guiding classroom approaches. The planning process is then overlaid with ten principles guiding evaluation and assessment. Clearly, the development of an effective primary school mathematics programme is a highly complex task.

I believe that a new strategy needs to be adopted if schools are to be successful in planning and implementing a mathematics curriculum which is capable of meeting the demands of tomorrow's world. It is interesting to compare the aims, goals and objectives for mathematical education drawn up in 1976 by the Mathematical Association in a leaflet *Why, What and How?*[10] with the *Mathematics from 5 to 16*[11] publication a decade later. It is not in the least surprising that there is little difference either in intent or in vocabulary. If the focus is narrowed to consider the primary age range then there still remains little difference, and the detailed analysis in *Mathematics 5–11*[12] reinforces this view. This suggests that schools, local authorities and national bodies should now have little difficulty in establishing consensus over the purposes of mathematical education.

If difficulties do not lie in the initial phase of the curriculum process then we need to look elsewhere for the derivation of problems which are inhibiting the school from achieving the best possible results. The next stage is to consider the content needed to

Planning the Curriculum

attain the goals that have been set. The review undertaken earlier suggests that there is wide variation of content and in some schools a reluctance to amend the traditional subject matter of primary mathematics in order to take on the new content needed to appreciate the basis of modern technology and use it effectively. Whatever the reasons for the reluctance to change, there can be little doubt that pressures from children, from parents and from employers will bring about the required change in content. Thus the teacher needs to adjust and to be successful, has to be confident with the new material and fully appreciative of its place and relationship with other mathematical constructs. This leads me to identify a factor of the greatest importance and one to which I will return — teacher confidence.

The nature and definition of the new content is not easy to determine. At all costs the top-down model which reflects a secondary examination led process must be avoided. Such a model would lead to a narrow and restricted mathematical experience.

In many cases primary schools will already be tied to a particular scheme or set of textbooks and new content may have to compete, and may conflict, with the current mathematics curriculum. There will be times when a school may be able to rethink its whole mathematics curriculum, in which case a recent publication by the Mathematical Association may help. A series of discussion papers[13] has been developed which are intended to guide a group of teachers through the necessary stages in order to reach a decision about a new scheme or in adopting a new textbook series. *Discussion Paper 3* focusses on content and whilst it does not, and is not, intended to set out a perfect curriculum content it does draw attention to the range of content that needs to be considered. Indeed, it goes further in that considering such related issues has the environmental, application of the content, sequencing and the need for additional material involved in the analysis. Figure 1 below taken from the material shows the main points to be taken into account when developing a mathematics curriculum.

The Figure has been developed to show the main points to be considered in an analysis of the mathematical differences between primary mathematics texts.[14]

The earlier discussion papers in the Mathematical Association publication guide the school in identifying its general aims and refining these to specify the purposes of the mathematics curriculum. The publication material also helps the school to clarify its teaching methods. The discussion paper indicates that there is some

5

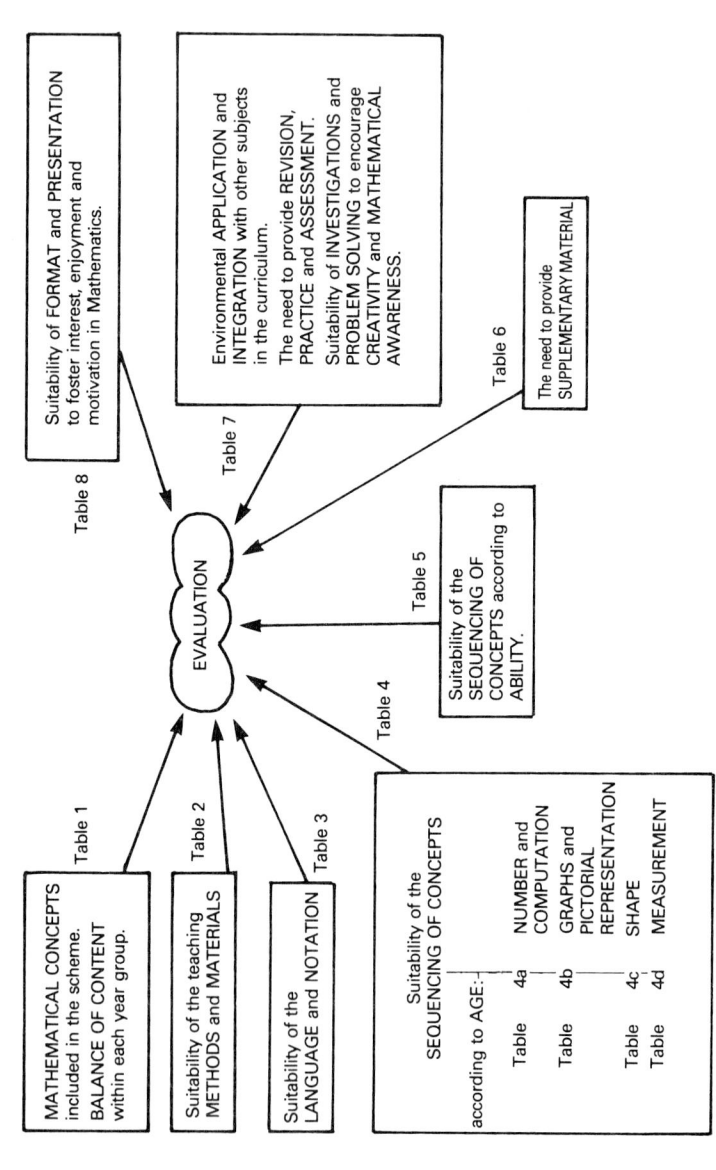

Figure 1: Chart to show the major points to be considered in an analysis of the mathematical differences between primary texts

Planning the Curriculum

freedom of choice, and a recognition that individual schools will meet the challenge of educating children mathematically in different ways. I believe strongly that this is right and therefore do not suggest a strict adherence to one specific source or textbook for curriculum content. HMI publications are also intended as guides and do not form prescriptive packages of curriculum ready to be taken off the shelf and used.

Turning now from identifying the content of the curriculum as one area of uncertainty, what other aspects of the curriculum process cause unease? Following the establishment of the content the curriculum planner's next task is to order the material and identify the best match of teaching method and approach to the mathematical concept involved. It is this link which evidence points to as being weak. For example the Primary Survey[15] found:

> There was a tendency in a number of classes to use individual work-card assignments when it would have been more appropriate to draw the group together to work from the blackboard or from a textbook. (para 5.54)
>
> Too great a reliance on the use of individual assignment cards. (para 5.54)
>
> Ideas common to two subjects were seldom linked in the work which children did in either subject; much more could be done in this way. (para 5.63)

Further evidence is found in the Cockcroft Report[16] and is well worth summarizing here as this issue of methodology and approach is essential to effective curriculum planning and implementation:

> The primary mathematics curriculum should enrich children's aesthetic and linguistic experience, provide them with the means of exploring their environment and develop their powers of logical thought, in addition to equipping them with the numerical skills which would be a powerful tool for later work and study. The primary years ought also to be seen as worthwhile in themselves — a time during which doors are opened onto a wide range of experiences. Practical work is essential throughout the primary years.[17]

A range of teaching methods is available to the teacher

— direct expositions
— discussion

— repetition and reinforcement
— practical and investigational work
— problem solving.

The difficulty lies in matching the technique to the content and to the prevailing circumstances. Furthermore their overall balance, say over a six-week period, is also important. It will involve consideration of the teaching methods being adopted in other subjects over the same period. This calls for a high level of skill in planning and an extensive knowledge of the material to be presented across the whole range of the curriculum. I believe it is this process which is at the heart of the complexity of the primary teacher's task.

The White Paper *Teaching Quality* highlights the crucial skills involved in the teaching process and exemplifies the point with reference to mathematics

> The value of a good match between the training and task of teachers is widely recognized. In November 1976 a Royal Society Report wrote — 'During his professional life, a teacher of mathematics may influence for good or ill the attitudes to mathematics of several thousand young people and decisively affect many of their career choices.' All pupils should have the opportunity of studying mathematics with enthusiastic and well qualified teachers.[18]

Whilst the Paper goes on to stress that government policy will be directed towards enhancing the quality of teachers in training it nevertheless recognized that mathematics, unlike science, is a central element in courses of training for primary teaching but often the most difficult for students. The basis for this observation is not given nor yet a proposal for resolving the problem other than to suggest an increase in the number of students taking mathematics as a main subject. Recent years have shown this policy to be barren and there has been a falling off in the numbers following main subject mathematics. The solution must be found from adopting other strategies.

Part of the folklore of mathematical education suggests that many children do not enjoy the subject or are afraid of it. There is also evidence that girls do not perform as well as boys in mathematics. Putting these two factors together and noting that the vast majority of students training for primary teaching are women then some appreciation of the size of the problem can be made. It is unlikely that there will be a sudden and dramatic reversal of the

Planning the Curriculum

trend of specialists coming forward for training and therefore answers to the difficulties must be found from within the system as it stands. The importance of mathematics is continually stressed and the subject together with language and reading development dominate the primary curriculum. Parents set great store on achievement in these curriculum areas and value them more highly than any others. I believe that this elevation of the subject to its 'five star' rating may have much to do with the fear, demotivation and worry shown by many children. In a rather similar way its high level of importance may well induce in teachers a lack of confidence, a tendency to play safe, and so adopt well tried methods and content. Thus the mathematical education of children becomes inhibited by a range of psychological pressures which are unrelated to the actual task in hand.

The approach to primary science appears to be somewhat different. Primarily the children are enthusiastic and well motivated. The subject is glamorous, has relevance to everyday life and indeed appears to be responsible for much that is valued in our present society. The majority of teachers on the other hand probably start from a weaker knowledge base than they do in mathematics. Perhaps it is their readiness to admit their weakness, their willingness to learn and to adopt a wider range of teaching approaches because these are traditional to the subject that greater progress appears to be being achieved in science.

I would argue that this more realistic approach by teachers together with the removal of the inhibiting pressures of 'importance' are necessary if progress is to be made to improve mathematical education. How might this be done? The rapid developments in microtechnology have led to an enormous change in the last five years in the provision of calculators and computer controlled instruments. Thus an account for a meal at one of the national roadside restaurant chains is arrived at by the cashier inputting the menu numbers and the till derives the bill as well as recording the items and providing a stock control facility for the management. This is just one example of many that readers will be aware of. Recognition of the real situation prevailing in the environment, without even taking into account future developments, must suggest that the proposals contained in the Cockcroft Report are already becoming dated, and similarly the justification in terms of relevance of much that is in *Mathematics from 5 to 16* is lessened.

An opportunity could be taken to consider the primary mathematics curriculum in two parts. The first part containing the essential elements in terms of knowledge and skills for basic numeracy and spatial awareness. The second section to be more open with greater freedom for the school to choose curriculum content but with the common intention of meeting the generally agreed aims and purposes of mathematical education. Such a development would have the purpose of reducing the tensions discussed earlier concerning the important and essential core.

It would be a smaller portion of curriculum, more basic and therefore with an increased likelihood of being achieved more readily. The second part would be much more akin to the science curriculum and the approach adopted could reflect an investigatory mode. The circumstances surrounding this section of the mathematics curriculum can be relaxed and create opportunities for experimentation in both content and teaching style. By removing some of the weight of responsibility from the teacher, in that this part of the syllabus is seen as extension material, it may well encourage a greater dialogue between teachers and a willingness to consult and seek help in the development of topics where the teacher feels less confident.

I believe that this proposal to divide the mathematics curriculum into two identifiable parts provides an opportunity for a total reappraisal of the whole primary curriculum. Within the subject itself there is the immediate task of separation. This will lead to a close scrutiny of the whole content with each element being considered in terms of its justification for inclusion and then its placing as core syllabus or extension material. When this is completed the syllabuses can be looked at in terms of teaching methods. The extension material will provide increased opportunities to look at cross curriculur possibilities and hence may lead to different approaches being adopted. This will have a further spin-off in that attention will be focussed on other curriculum subjects or areas of experience to see what opportunities exist for the introduction of a mathematical element. It has been remarked and written many times before that children do not think in terms of subjects nor yet does their everyday experience present life in terms of subjects. The deliberate presentation of mathematics in an integrated subject form may provide the pupil with a more encouraging and relevant experience. Hopefully this will lead to more effective learning and increased motivation.

So far I have presented some of the issues underlying the process of planning a mathematics curriculum that will take account

Planning the Curriculum

of the future and at least try to eradicate some of the past difficulties. I now turn to the curriculum planning process itself.

It is realistic to plan for a seven-year cycle of curriculum development for the whole curriculum of a school with attention being given in the intervening years to specific areas of experience or subjects. Numerous models and diagrams have been developed to help schools and teachers plan, develop and assess the curriculum. I find the application of a model useful as a guide to ensure that all the major perspectives of the process are involved. The recognition of the requirement to regularly reconsider the whole process, albeit over a seven-year period, does suggest a continuous rather than a linear model. The diagram below provides some guide for curriculum development.

Figure 2: A model for staged curriculum planning

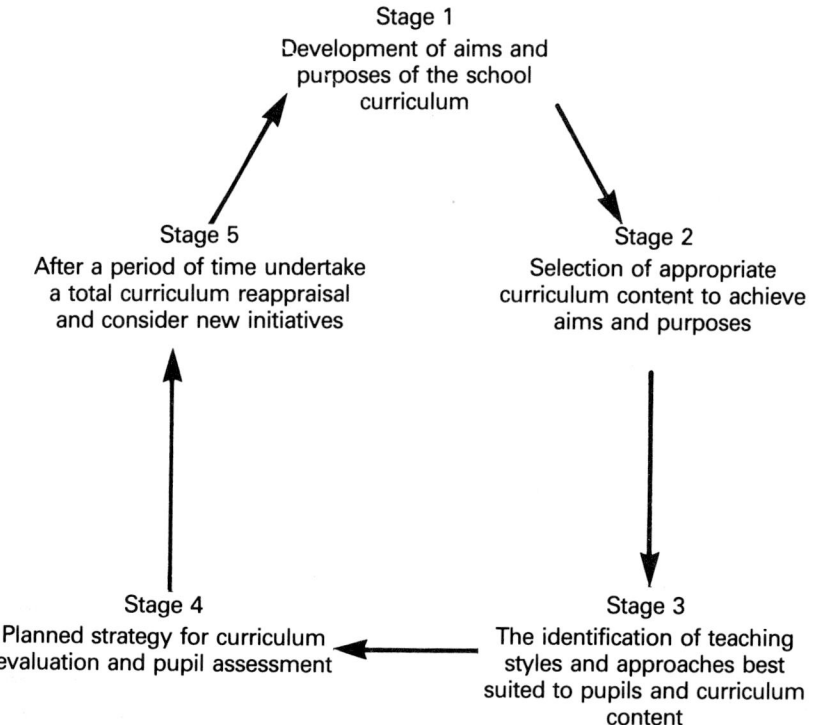

Michael Preston

The same model can be easily adapted for the development of a subject curriculum within the framework of the whole school curriculum. The mathematics curriculum can be seen to be a part of the whole and easily represented on a Venn diagram.

Figure 3: The relationship of mathematical education to the whole curriculum

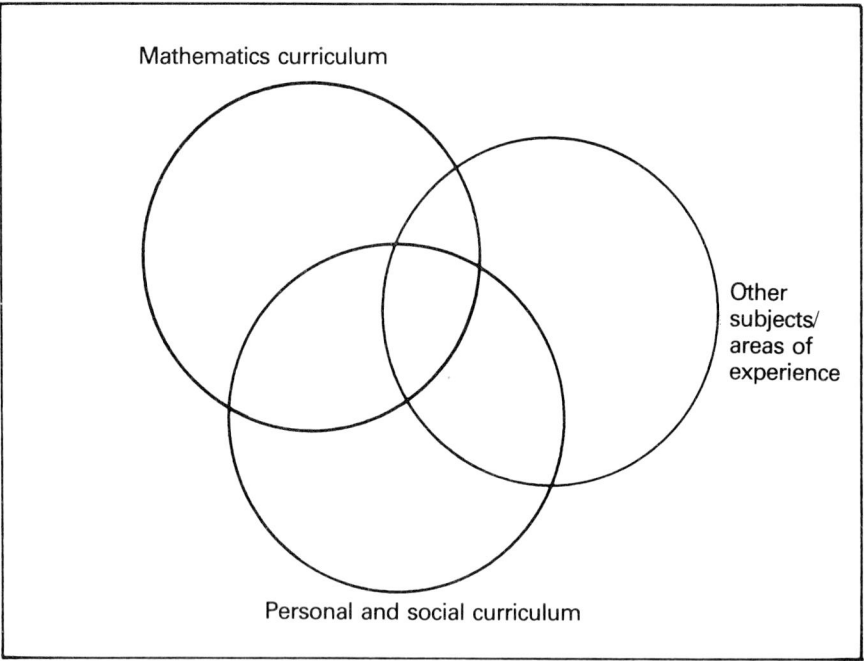

Once stage 1 of the model (figure 2) has been evolved for the school then the team responsible for the mathematics curriculum can reinterpret stage 1 in terms of the aims and purposes of the mathematics curriculum. The curriculum planning team then follow through the remaining stages. At each point it is essential to have effective liaison with staff responsible for other aspects of the whole curriculum for, as the Venn diagram shows, there is, and indeed there must be, intersection with other learning experiences being presented to pupils.

The remaining chapters of this book are designed to focus on the major perspectives that need to be considered when a school is planning its mathematics curriculum and they also identify where help and other resources can be found. The Mathematics Association publication[19] based on choosing a mathematics scheme draws

Planning the Curriculum

all the various steps together in its final section and presents a very useful summary in the form of a diagram. This is reproduced below and if the centre word 'scheme' is replaced by 'curriculum implementation' then considerable value for the curriculum planning exercise can be gained.

An inspection of figure 4 immediately underlines the complexity of curriculum planning and shows the degree of consultation and management decision making that needs to be undertaken if effective learning is to follow. This process is time-consuming and can only be followed over an extended period if it is not to detract from the teachers day-to-day efficiency in carrying forward the work of the classroom.

The six factors surrounding 'curriculum implementation' all affect major management decisions on the use of the basic resources of the school in terms of cost, staff time and curriculum materials. This analysis reinforces the point made earlier that a full revision of a subject curriculum or the whole school curriculum can only take place every five or seven years. It is particularly important to consider the criticisms of mathematical education reviewed earlier in this chapter and set these alongside the two factors — staff development and support for staff. Whether the strategy proposed earlier of a two-part mathematics curriculum, or some other plan is devised to meet the criticisms, the implication for the in-service education programme for teachers is significant. It is interesting to note that the recently published House of Commons Report[20] recognizes this factor in a very strongly worded recommendation:

> We recommend that all primary schools should be required to operate according to development plans agreed with the governing body and LEA ... We believe that such a requirement would provide a good opportunity for heads and teachers to use their initiative and imagination; to influence the form and content of INSET ... The plan should be a whole school plan to which all teachers should contribute as class teachers and to a greater or lesser degree as coordinators; it should act as a unifying force in the work of staff and children. (para 13.15)

This powerful statement places the responsibility for curriculum planning and implementation firmly in the hands of the school. The expectations from a thorough consideration of the curriculum and the evolution of a staff development plan fit well with the

13

Michael Preston

Figure 4: Interrelated factors in implementing a new scheme

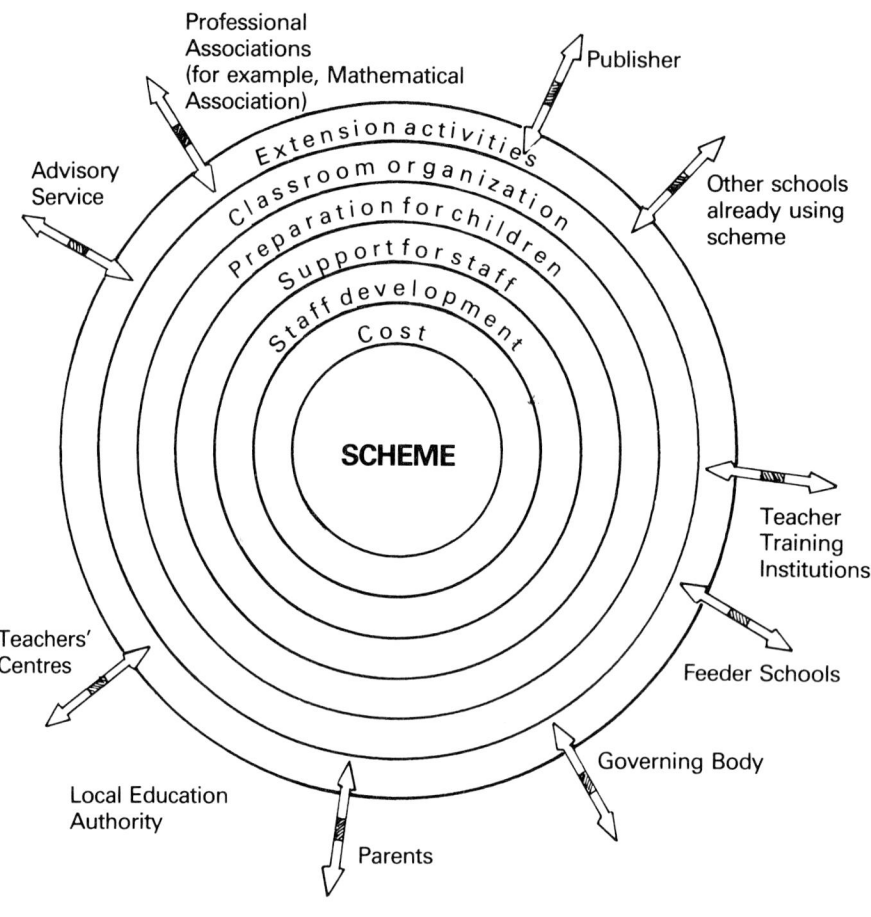

Planning the Curriculum

arguments and conclusions that I have tried to consider in this chapter.

Summary

Recent reviews of mathematical education suggest that much of the syllabus content is sound but weakness lies in the transmission of knowledge and in some negative attitudes developed by children to mathematics. The expectations of mathematical education by the Cockcroft Committee, the DES and HMI are higher than can be delivered by the teaching force as it currently exists and with its present level of support.

A new strategy is needed to develop fresh thinking and to work out approaches to the teaching of mathematics that teachers will be able to cope with, and respond to, with confidence. The new strategy must achieve higher levels of attainment and enhanced interest and motivation.

A process model of curriculum planning was developed and consideration given to the major dimensions that need to be involved if effective implementation is to be achieved. The importance of mathematical education as an integral part of the whole school curriculum was stressed throughout and this importance was underlined by the need for a well structured and managed school development plan.

Notes and References

1 COCKCROFT, WH (1982) *Report of the Committee of Enquiry into the Teaching of Mathematics in Schools: Mathematics Counts*, London, HMSO.
2 DEPARTMENT OF EDUCATION AND SCIENCE (1985) *Mathematics from 5 to 16*, London, HMSO.
3 SCHOOLS COUNCIL (1960) *Curriculum Bulletin No 1: Mathematics*, London, HMSO.
4 DEPARTMENT OF EDUCATION AND SCIENCE (1978) *Primary Education in England — A Survey by HM Inspectors of Schools*, London, HMSO.
5 COCKCROFT, WH (1982) *op cit*, para 285.
6 *Ibid*, para 306.
7 DEPARTMENT OF EDUCATION AND SCIENCE (1985) *op cit*.
8 *Ibid*, criteria 3, 4 and 7.
9 *Ibid*, principles 2, 3, 5 and 9.

10 MATHEMATICAL ASSOCIATION (1976) *Why, What and How*, Leicester, Mathematical Association.
11 DEPARTMENT OF EDUCATION AND SCIENCE (1979) *Mathematics 5–11: A Handbook of Suggestions*, London, HMSO.
12 *Ibid*.
13 PRESTON, M et al (1986) *Choosing a Primary School Mathematics Textbook or Scheme*, Leicester, Mathematical Association.
14 *Ibid*, discussion paper 3.
15 DEPARTMENT OF EDUCATION AND SCIENCE (1978) *op cit*.
16 COCKCROFT, WH (1982) *op cit*.
17 *Ibid*, paras 287 and 289.
18 DEPARTMENT OF EDUCATION AND SCIENCE (1983) *Teaching Quality* (Cmnd 8836), chapter 3, paras 28 and 32, London, HMSO.
19 PRESTON, M et al (1986) *op cit*.
20 HOUSE OF COMMONS (1986) *Third Report from the Education, Science and Arts Committee — Achievement in Primary Schools, Volume 1 (40–1)*, London, HMSO.

Teaching and Learning Mathematics in the Primary School

David Owen

Introduction

Throughout history there has been conflict between mathematics seen as a subject growing out of economic and social necessity and the view that mathematics has a purity which transcends mere practicality. Euclid, when asked by a slave what he would get by learning geometry, offered him a coin of little value so that he could gain from what he had learned! More recently, Hardy, in *A Mathematician's Apology*[1], said, 'I have never done anything *useful*. No discovery of mine has made, or is likely to make, directly or indirectly, for good or ill, the least difference to the amenity of the world'. Robert Recorde,[2] writing in 1540, takes a contrary position in noting that:

> If number be lacking it maketh men dumbe
> So that to most questions they must answer mum.

Mathematicians, however great, can miss the point as easily as the rest of us. Much of Robert Recorde's arithmetical work became less useful with the development of logarithms in the eighteenth century, and totally redundant with the advent of modern calculating devices. In contrast, Hardy's work does have practical applications in the modern world and may have even more powerful influences in the future.

Mathematics is as 'man-made' as polystyrene but, through its abstract nature, structures and patterns can be produced which are applicable in a wide variety of contexts. The *usefulness* of particular branches of the subject are totally dependent upon social, cultural and historical contexts but *enjoyment* of the subject is not governed by the same constraints. The challenge for the teacher is to ensure that the mathematical experiences offered to the children are more like this:

Figure 1

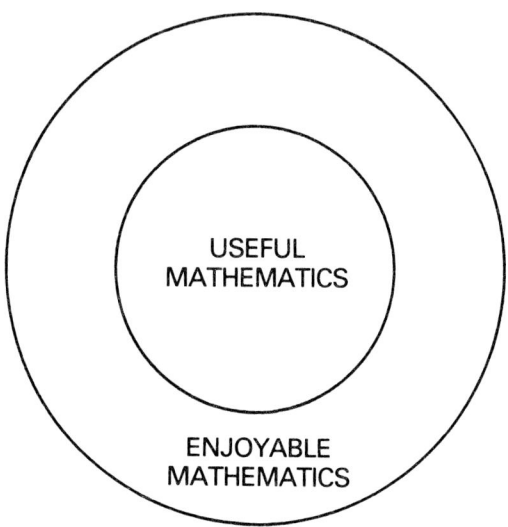

than this:

Figure 2

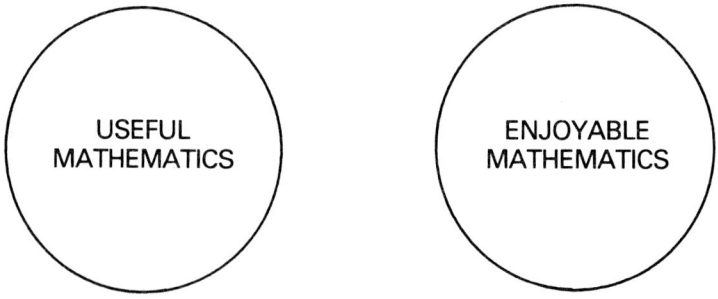

This chapter attempts to raise issues for teaching and learning mathematics through a consideration of particular happenings in both the adult world and the world of the child.

Teaching and Learning Mathematics

The Basics

It is interesting to reflect on the emotional responses to the term 'the basics' both from those who insist that 'these must be taught' to those who reject a 'back to the basics' movement. Together with the Cockcroft Report[3], *Mathematics 5–11*[4] and *Mathematics from 5 to 16*[5], I must, of course, find myself firmly in the latter camp. However, I am only there because of a desire to *redefine* the basics! It would not be possible to attempt such a redefinition within a chapter of this length and it is strongly recommended that the reader refers to the above publications, since they are entirely concerned with detailing up-to-date views of 'basic' aims, objectives, content, teaching methods and assessment procedures in mathematics education.

Example A

Some time ago, when I was still a smoker, I stopped at a garage near my home and bought ten cigarettes for 63p and returned to my car. Realizing that the day was to be spent in a smoke-filled room with others suffering the same addiction, I returned and asked the lady who had served me if I could have twenty cigarettes instead. I was frozen to the spot by the look which I received!

'I suppose so', she said, and proceeded, on a sheet of paper, carefully to subtract 63p from £1.25. Eventually, she asked me for the additional 62p. I realized then that the source of her unpleasantness was the fact that she would have to perform a mathematical calculation. I was amazed that she needed to resort to pencil and paper. The lady was *not* the archetypal 'slip of a girl — straight out of school — unable to do simple arithmetic'. She was a mature lady, well into her fifties, who had no doubt been subjected to years of practice in calculating!

Implications for the Classroom

1. It is essential that children develop mental facility with number, combined with the effective use of devices for calculating. Turning *children* into calculating machines is no longer necessary. Even when there was some necessity to do so, many people failed to become effective calculators.

2 The mathematical provision in the classroom should be such that it provides children with opportunities to use mathematics to explain the world around them rather than to obscure it. For the majority of adults, mathematics acts like frosted glass rather than a high-resolution microscope. The lady in this example could not bring into focus all the mathematics she had been taught in order to handle a very simple problem.

Example B

During the last two or three years, whenever I have found children *successfully* tackling 'long' multiplications I have invited them to tell me the result of multiplying one of the numbers by ten or a hundred (so, for example, if they had been successful in multiplying 347 by 34 I would ask them to multiply 347 by 10 or, perhaps, 34 by 100). Although I have not kept records in detail, something like 75 per cent of top juniors able to perform the relatively unimportant long multiplication algorithm *are not able* to deal with the really important digit shift involved in the questions which I posed.

Implications for the Classroom

1 Real or imagined pressure from parents, the headteacher, the adviser, HMI, the governors, politicians, the media and secondary school teachers can lead to a situation where those things that are relatively easy to assess by paper and pencil tests (mainly skills) are emphasized at the expense of those things which are more difficult to assess (mainly concepts and the application of knowledge).

The Cockcroft Report coined the phrase 'the seven year gap' to indicate the great differences which can exist between individual children in their understanding of mathematics. It is my view that the content in mathematics has often been determined by that which can be absorbed by the most able. The hierarchical neatness of the subject has made it possible to set targets and then attempt to get children 'on'. The end product has been that at all levels (from reception to undergraduate) children and young people have been offered too much, too soon in terms of mathematical content. Furthermore, the mathematics that children have been offered is way beyond what is required as a 'social and economic necessity' and certainly contains little of the 'purity' mentioned at the start of this chapter. What we have had is rote learning, lack of understanding, boredom and fear.

Looking for 'Solutions'

It is important to note at this point the great improvements which have taken place in the teaching of mathematics in primary schools in the last twenty years. The work of Miss Biggs, HMI and of the Nuffield Mathematics Project led to a greater emphasis on:

— practical work in mathematics;
— the need for children to understand the mathematics they are using;
— the broadening of the curriculum away from arithmetic towards mathematics;
— linking the subject with other areas of the curriculum.

These developments have brought about great improvements in children's (and teachers'!) attitudes toward the subject.

Teachers work far harder now than they have ever done to try to maintain and improve upon the developments which have already taken place. Much of what goes on in an individual classroom depends on the overall planning for the school and the degree of mutual support which staff can offer. However, the individual teacher can edge forward the quality of his or her own individual provision for mathematics by responding to the suggestions given in paragraph 243 of the Cockcroft Report, where it is advocated that teachers should make use of the following teaching styles:

— exposition (teaching individuals, groups, or a class);
— discussion (between teachers and children and between children and children);
— practice in fundamental skills;
— problem-solving (including applications across the curriculum and to everyday situations);
— appropriate practical work (ie practical work with a purpose, with meaning to the child, and at the right level);
— investigational work (explorations either individually or in groups).

Whilst each of these elements is equally important, I have

chosen in the rest of this chapter to concentrate upon investigational work, problem solving and discussion in the classroom since these elements represent the greatest challenge and change for many, if not most, teachers.

Investigatory Work

The terms 'investigational or investigatory work' and 'problem-solving', whilst helpful in many ways, cause two major difficulties:

— no two people seem to share definitions of the terms;
— the words tend to cause panic among teachers.

In this section I offer some thoughts on investigatory work and in the next section some examples on problem-solving. To avoid confusion I make no attempt to define either term! The panic mentioned above is induced by visions of geoboards, open-endedness, leaps into the unknown, generalizations, lack of structure, and the like. Help is at hand through many publications concerned with investigatory work in mathematics. An excellent (and cheap) starting point can be made by purchasing the *Maths Extra*[6] materials from Avon LEA. I can also highly recommend *Sources of Mathematical Discovery*[7] by Mottershead and *Mathematical Activities*[8] by Bolt. However, there is another very important issue at stake. We must avoid the eighties' equivalent of the sixties', 'We do practical maths on Friday afternoons'. The Cockcroft Report and *Mathematics from 5 to 16* helpfully make the point that investigatory/exploratory/problem-solving approaches could and should be brought to bear on simple standard pieces of work. The examples below are intended to illustrate this approach and some of the issues which arise.

Example A

A teacher of a class of top infants and first year juniors in a school with a high proportion of socially deprived children asked her children to make up 'sums' which gave the answer six. They were allowed to use any of the four rules but not surprisingly most settled for addition and subtraction. The following day one boy in the class asked the teacher if he could 'make up any sums I like'. She was delighted, since the child had a history of being extremely disruptive. Furthermore, his level of achievement (in a class of low achievers) was seen as very low indeed. For example, a recent reading test indicated a reading age of 5 years, 4 months for a child of chronological age 8 years, 5 months (reading quotient 63). The fifty-eight additions produced by the child are reproduced on pages 24 and 25.

Implications for the Classroom

1 The child was greatly motivated by the open-ended nature of this task.
2 The quality of the work was way above that which the child normally produced. He did things which the teacher did not know he could tackle. Although, admittedly, the only standardized test to which the child had been subjected was a reading test, this exercise raises questions about the misplaced faith which so many people have in assessment materials of this type.
3 The quantity of work produced gave a tremendous boost to the child's confidence.
4 This is a good example of the suggestion made on page 49 of *Mathematics from 5 to 16* (paragraph 5.13) that there is much to be gained from using assessment procedures which allow pupils to show *their* capabilities. I quote part of paragraph 5.13. below.

The following tasks offer much more scope:

> Find different calculations or types of calculation which have an answer equal to 36.
> Find different equations which have one root, $x = 10$.

These questions have many right answers and so such questions allow pupils to explore many different possibilities. Indeed each question could be a complete half-hour test in itself and could well reveal more about the pupils' abilities than, say, twenty different questions of a closed nature.

Although, in our example, there had been no intention to assess in the formal sense, the teacher was able to use the child's work to give her a picture of his grasp of some concepts but not others. It is also possible to obtain a view of the strategies which he has used. Consider for a moment:

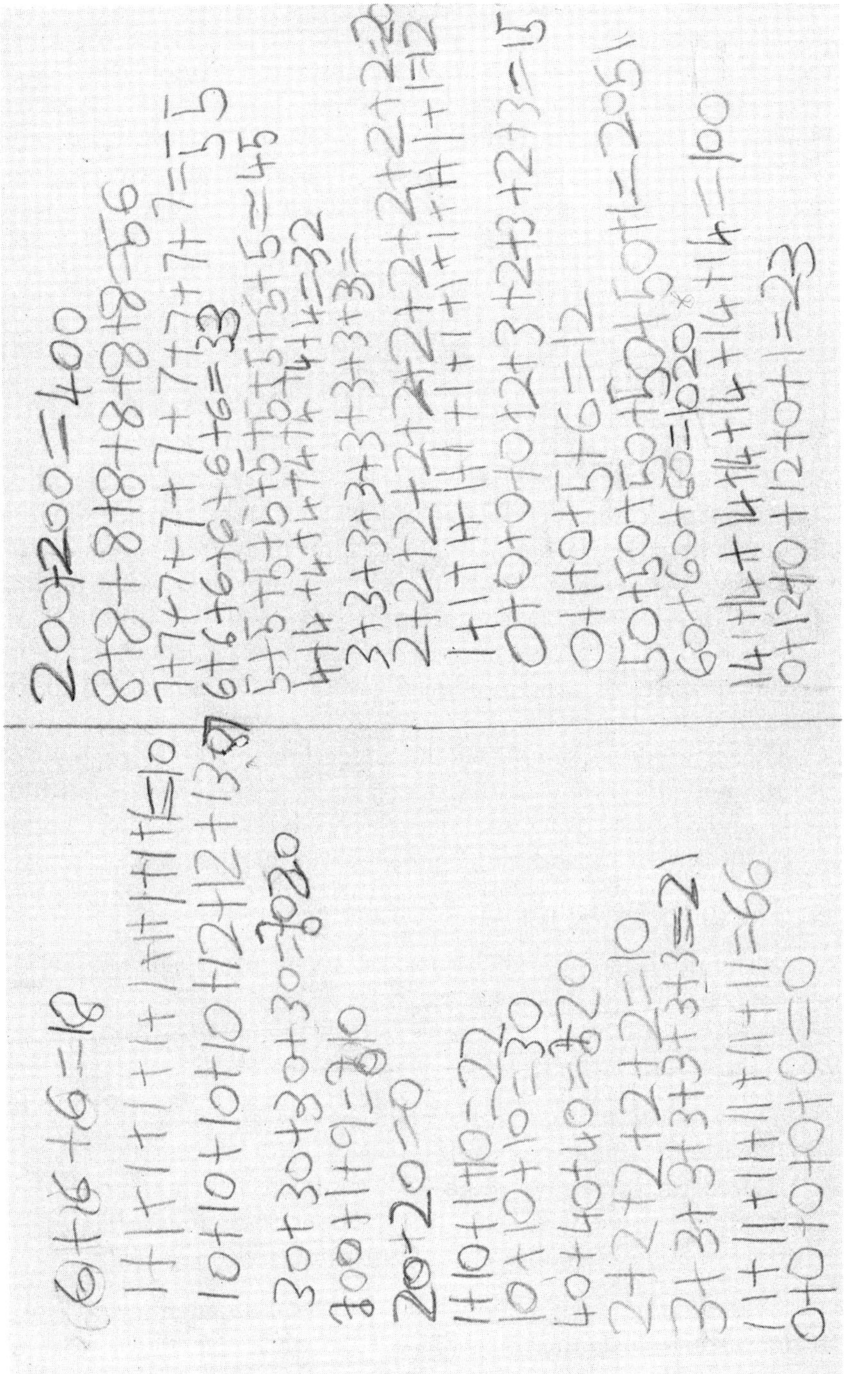

David Owen

$200+200=400$
$8+8+8+8+8=96$ [likely 8×12=96 style, reading: $8+8+8+8+8+8+8+8+8+8+8+8=96$]
$7+7+7+7+7+7+7=55$ [likely $7+7+7+7+7=35$... reading as written]
$6+6+6+6+6+6=33$
$5+5+5+5+5+5+5+5+5=45$
$4+4+4+4+4+4+4+4=32$
$3+3+3+3+3+3+3+3+3+3+3=$
$2+2+2+2+2+2+2+2+2+2+2=22$
$1+1+1+1+1+1+1+1+1+1+1+1=12$
$0+0+0+0+0+0+0+0+0+0+0+0=0$ [reading unclear]

$10+10+5+6=12$ [reading: $1+10+5+6=$]
$10+10+5+6=$
$50+50+50+50+50=205$ [likely $50+50+50+50+5=205$]
$60+60+60=1020$ [unclear]
$14+14+14+14+14+14+14=100$
$12+10+12+10=$
$1+0+1+0+1+0=23$ [unclear]

$6+6+6=18$
$1+1+1+1+1+1+1+1+1+1=10$
$10+10+10+10+12+12+13=87$
$30+30+30+30=7020$ [unclear]
$300+1+9=310$
$20+20=40$
$1+10+110=22$
$10+10+10=30$
$40+40+40=120$
$2+2+2+2+2=10$
$3+3+3+3+3+3+3=21$
$1+1+1+1+1+1+1+1+1=99$ [reading unclear]
$0+0+0+0+0+0+0+0+0=0$

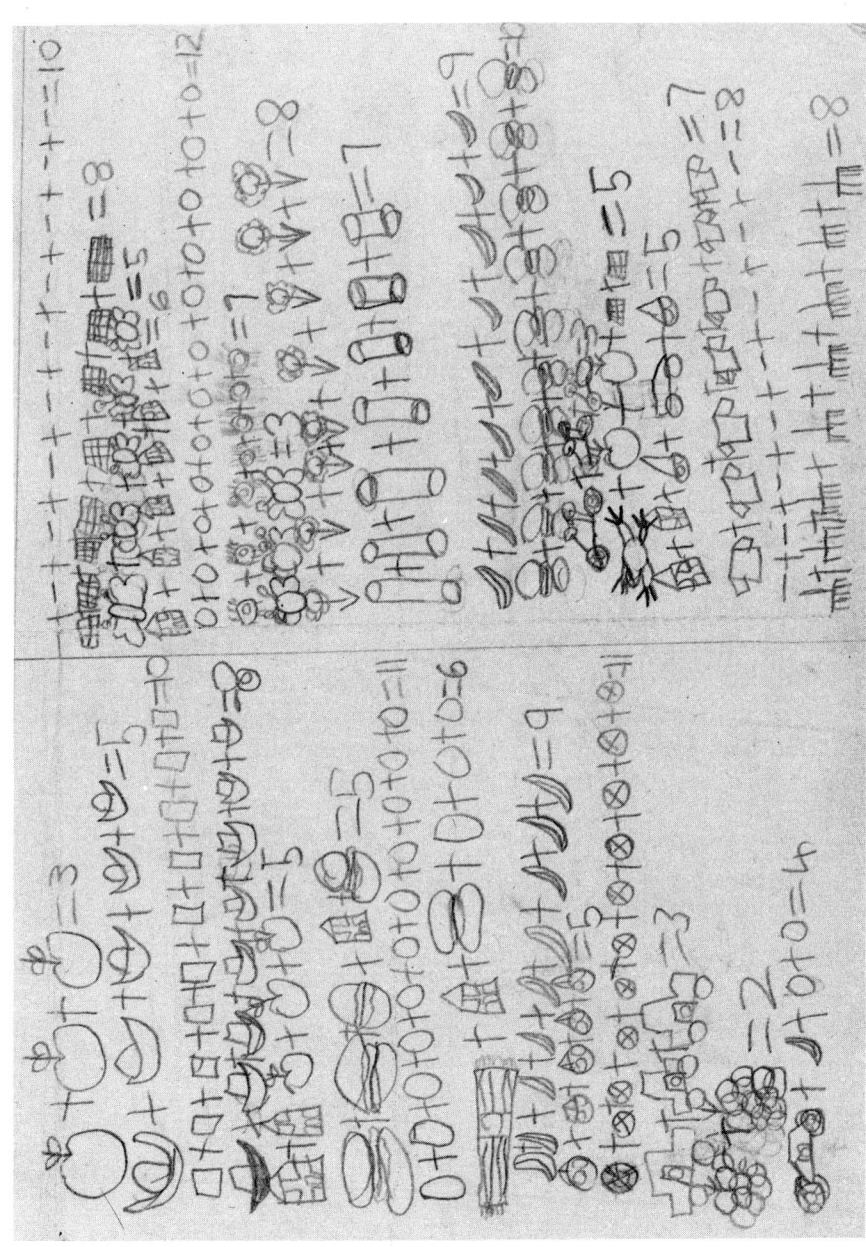

(a) Why does $0 + 0 + 0 + 0 + 0 = 0$ but
$0 + 0 + 0 + 0 + 0 + 0 + 0 + 0 + 0 + 0 + 0 + 0 = 12$?
(b) The jump made from
$8 + 8 + 8 + 8 + 8 + 8 + 8 = 56$
to $7 + 7 + 7 + 7 + 7 + 7 + 7 + 7 + 7 = 55$
(More than a guess I would suggest. More like a slightly off-beam strategy which has given an incorrect result.)
(c) $14 + 14 + 14 + 14 + 14 + 14 + 14 = 100$
(Probably hard luck, but it could be an estimate.)
(d) $50 + 50 + 50 + 50 + 50 + 1 = 2051$
(Faulty grasp of place value.)

Example B

In a particular school children from the third and fourth years are placed in three sets for mathematics. When visiting the set containing the children designated as the least able I asked the busy teacher if I might go around the class and talk to individual children and groups. At first I assumed that the children had been invited to make a shape and divide it in half since the first half a dozen children had done exactly that and were carefully cutting out their shapes to make a display. Then I came upon a boy who had made this shape:

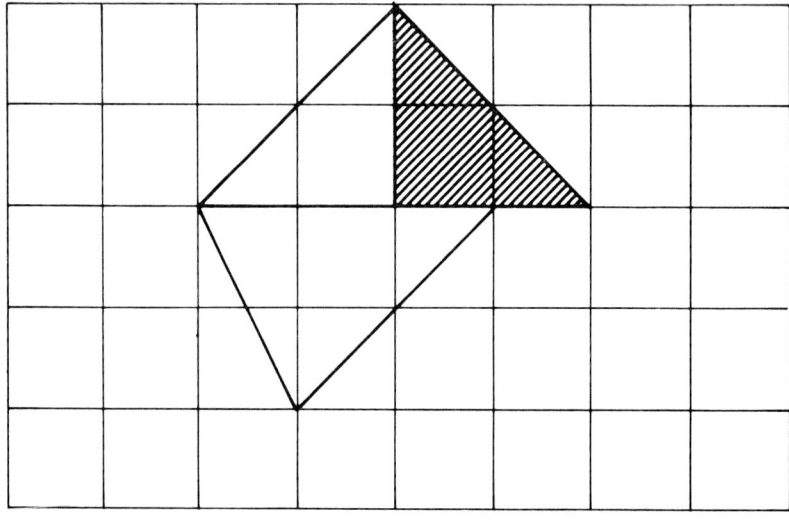

Teaching and Learning Mathematics

When I asked him what he was doing he pointed to the shaded part and said, 'This part is two-sevenths'. I must admit that before I had checked I had supposed that the child had given me the first fraction that came into his head. When I realized that he was correct I asked him why it was two-sevenths and with great panache he proved it by counting squares.

I was delighted, and so was his teacher when I told her. Some of the things she had to say were interesting. 'I'm not very sure about teaching mathematics — I've only taken infants before' and 'Of course, he shouldn't be in this set, but he doesn't like things like multiplication'.

I put her mind at rest and told her I thought the activity was splendid and provided this child with an opportunity to show his capabilities.

Implications for the Classroom

1 Despite the fact that setting as an organizational arrangement receives some degree of support from the Cockcroft Report (para 350), I would suggest that this example illustrates dramatically one of the major difficulties associated with allocating children to particular sets at the age of 10 (ie, it is very difficult indeed to get the assessment anywhere near correct).

   Other problems associated with setting include the impact on:

   — the pupils (both emotionally and academically);
   — the curriculum (more likely to be subject-based);
   — the teaching of mathematics (less likely to be integrated with other areas of the curriculum);
   — teaching styles (since some teachers will imagine they are working with homogenous groups there is a tendency to have an over emphasis upon class teaching).

2 Different branches of the subject are often viewed in quite different ways by teachers. For example, for many years long division (now officially buried by *Mathematics from 5 to 16*) had a much higher status than knowledge about the geometry of the circle. Consider for a moment the repercussions of a lack of enthusiasm for multiplication at the age of 9 or 10!

3 It is important in the classroom to develop integration *within* mathematics, as well as establishing links with other areas of the

curriculum. The child in this example was working in number (fractions) and the measures (area) within a geometrical context.

Problem-Solving

Mathematics 5–16 indicates quite clearly that problem-solving is not the same as giving children 'sums with words' from a textbook. When I was a child of primary school age I greatly impressed my teacher by being very quick to finish the 'problems' pages in my textbook. Having completed, say, forty 'mechanical' multiplications on the left-hand side of a double page, I could be quite certain that I would face twenty or thirty multiplication problems on the right-hand side of the page! Therefore I didn't bother to read the words, I simply multiplied whatever numbers were given.

Present day textbooks, apart from the layout, have changed little in their approach to problems. I am a strong advocate of 'real problem solving' using the term in a way similar to that coined by the Open University in the excellent *Mathematics Across the Curriculum* course[9]. Real problem-solving aims to involve groups of children (perhaps a whole class or a whole school) in a problem which is of importance to them and, if and when it is solved, will have outcomes of benefit to them. Work is often long-term, requires that the children work together cooperatively, and involves them in first-hand experiences. It is almost certain that the children's work will spread genuinely across the curriculum. It is strongly suggested that the reader refers to the course books for *Mathematics Across the Curriculum*. In a short chapter it would be inappropriate to describe in detail examples of real problem-solving but it is possible to consider some simple problems which have arisen in real contexts and which illustrate various important matters.

Example A: The New Kettle

At a party a friend noted a worthy but expensive and inefficient attempt at safety-consciousness. This involved the fitting of various fuses sequentially in the plug attached to a new kettle — the kettle blew the 3 amp and 5 amp fuses, but did not blow the 13 amp fuse. Several people suggested that a 10 amp fuse would have sufficed and when I asked four of them how they knew the responses were interesting and I give them below:

Teaching and Learning Mathematics

1. 'I knew — I'd just bought a similar kettle.'
2. 'I used the relationship W = VA (Watts = Voltage × Amps).'
   [The kettle had a rating of 2100 watts, therefore the formula gives
   $2100 = 240 \times A$
   $A = 2100 \div 240$
   $A = 10$ (approximately).]
3. 'I know that a 3kw (3000w) appliance requires a 13 amp fuse. Therefore a 1kw appliance would require a fuse of slightly more than 4 amps. Therefore a 2kw fire would require a 9 amp fuse, which I haven't got! Therefore I would fit a 10 amp fuse.'
4. '2100 watts is approximately two-thirds of 3kw. Therefore the fuse must be two-thirds of 13 amps, which is approximately 8 amps.'

Implications for the Classroom

You must not think that I ruin every party by asking people silly questions! However, there are a number of important issues arising from this incident.

1. There is rarely a unique way of approaching even the simplest of problems. Similarly, real life problems often do not have a single solution. It is not desperately serious that a 13 amp fuse was used and it would have been possible to have used a 9 amp, 11 amp or 12 amp fuse (assuming that these were readily available).
2. If you have checked the arithmetic you will have realized that $2100 \div 240$ is 8.75. It is important that children be given the opportunity to interpret results in the context of the problem (please see para 2.21., page 17 in *Mathematics from 5 to 16*).
3. It is useful to share with others our ways of thinking.
4. It is important to develop in children 'a feeling for number which permits sensible estimation and approximation' (para 33 of the Cockcroft Report).

David Owen

Example B: The Beano

One day, some years ago, my youngest son Daniel, who was then 9 years old, asked me if *The Beano* was around when I was a boy. When I replied in the affirmative, he asked whether it was available when Grandad was a boy. I didn't know and said to him, 'Why don't you find out?'.

'Sum's too hard!', was the reply.

'Don't worry', I said, 'we can use a calculator. What sum do we need to do?'.

'It's a sharing', he offered, confidently.

'Yes, it's a division', I noted somewhat pedantically, 'what do you have to divide by what?'.

'Well, it says issue 2090 at the top of the front page ...'.

Silence reigned for a little while. 'Is it 2090 divided by 365?'.

'Not unless you get it every day!', I pointed out. By this time, Michael, who is seventeen months older, had joined us and we explained our 'problem'. The two boys considered the matter for a while, then one of them said, 'I think it's 2090 divided by 7'.

I suggested that it was time for us to use the calculator and after doing this the boys decided that 298.5714 years did seem a bit much (after all, it would have meant that *The Beano* was first published before *The Observer* or *The Times*!).

At last, I was offered the correct calculation:
2090 ÷ 52 = 40.192307 years.

'Grandad's 68', said one of the boys, '*The Beano*'s only 40 years old'.

Clearly the problem had been solved, but out of interest I asked them what they thought the decimal part of 40.192307 years meant. The reply came in a flash, 'It's the weeks'. I was very surprised when the following process took place at the calculator. 40 was subtracted (leaving 0.192307). This was multiplied by 52 to give 9.999964 weeks, which was quickly seen to mean 10 weeks.

Implications for the Classroom

1 The problem was highly motivating because it was the child's own.
2 The adult played a vital but recessive role in the interaction, providing the children with the opportunity to think.
3 Even though I was the boys' father I was not very accurate in

my perceptions of how easy or hard they were likely to find particular ideas. Specifically, I never imagined that it would take quite so long to find out what 'sum' we needed to do, but on the other hand I was surprised at the rapidity with which 40.192307 years was converted to 40 years 10 weeks. Teachers who struggle with 'matching' work to the needs of individual children should be heartened by this. 'Matching' is a vital thing to attempt, but it will always be very much an approximate art.

4 The significance of the calculator in solving this problem should be noted. One of the many great benefits brought about by the availability of cheap calculating devices is that they provide the teacher with the opportunity to shift the work in the classroom away from 'Can I do this sum?' towards 'What sum do I need to do in this particular context?'. The calculator enables children to process real data.

5 A problem can often introduce children to new mathematical ideas. Similarly, the calculator can often provoke new thinking. This was almost certainly the first time the boys had seen time expressed as years and a decimal part of a year. The sowing of good seeds at school had probably led to effective handling of the situation. I suspect the thinking went something like this:

> 'I've just divided by 52 to change weeks to years. Therefore I must multiply by 52 to change the (decimal part of) years back to weeks'.

This firm grasp that multiplication is the inverse of division could only have come about through the provision of appropriate experiences at school.

The reader might like to try out our calculations to illustrate the point that calculators vary in the way they handle calculations and in the approximations used. Below I give the original calculations once again, together with the same calculations on two other (scientific) machines.

Machine 1	2090	÷	52	=	40.192307
		−	40	=	0.192307
		×	52	=	9.999964
Machine 2	2090	÷	52	=	40.192308
		−	40	=	0.192308
		×	52	=	10

David Owen

Machine 3   2090 ÷ 52 = 40.192308
                    − 40 = 0.1923076
                    × 52 = 9.9999999

    For further useful information on the use of calculators in the classroom, I would refer the reader to the *Calculators in the Primary School*[10] student pack from the Open University.

6 A significant factor in this problem is that not all the data is immediately available — a not uncommon factor in real life. We can imagine the textbook equivalent of this problem:

> If there are fifty-two weeks in the year and issue 2090 of *The Beano* has just been published, how old is the comic?.

In the textbook example the children merely have to decide what operation they have to use to associate 2090 and 52. The child who fails to realize that division is required will probably ascertain this fairly quickly by asking a friend or the teacher. No problem has been solved, it is merely another 'long' division in words.

7 As noted in *Mathematics from 5 to 16*, the process of starting with a real problem, abstracting and solving a corresponding mathematical problem, and then checking its solution in the practical situation, is often called mathematical modelling. Rather devastatingly, the mathematical model formed for *The Beano* is far from perfect! First of all, you may have noted that a year is, of course, fifty-two weeks one day long (and then there are leap years). Even more serious, is the fact, as I understand it from friends, the *The Beano* was published fortnightly during the war! Often, in real life, there is a need to refine mathematical models to reflect reality more accurately.

Example C: The Carpet

The following incident occurred about four years ago when my wife and I were buying a new carpet. I decided, after measuring the room, that 15′1″ of 12-foot broadloom would be adequate. Don't worry, I have been metricated, but most shops selling carpet have not! I also make no apologies for the meanness in establishing the length of the carpet required to the nearest inch!

Teaching and Learning Mathematics

In the car, on the way to the shop, we discussed the probable cost of the carpet, estimating this to be £200 (five yards by four yards with an estimated cost of £10 per square yard). In the shop we selected the carpet and waited patiently while the shop assistant struggled mentally, with pencil and paper and with a calculator before arriving at a price of £197.46. This was clearly of the right order and I paid for the carpet. However, as so much time had been taken on the calculation, on my return to the car I decided to check and discovered that I had been under-charged by 43p! Once again, in case the reader holds any prejudices I should point out that the shop assistant was late middle aged, male and very smartly dressed.

Implications for the Classroom

1 You might be surprised to learn that a carpet priced at £9.84 per square yard would cost £11.77 per square metre, hence the apparent conservatism of carpet shops.

   There is general agreement that children should be familiar with the common imperial units as well as the metric system and helpful comments are to be found on page 47 of *Mathematics 5–11* and paras 273–275 of the Cockcroft Report.

2 Para 4.9 of *Mathematics from 5 to 16* notes that:

> there is the practical work of measurement which needs to be done with a particular purpose in mind, whether as part of mathematical activities or in other subjects in the curriculum. Meaningless calculations involving measurements, such as the multiplication of 2 hours 27 minutes by 6, serve little useful purpose.

   Some of the purposes that I had in mind in measuring my room were to enable me:

   (a) To order the minimum amount of carpet consistent with actually covering the floor. The length of the room is, in fact, slightly under 15′ (one-inch was added as a 'safety margin'). It is interesting to speculate whether a carpet fitter measuring the room would have saved me money (by using 15′) or whether his margin of safety would have been rounded up to 15′3″.
   (b) To estimate the cost of the carpet.
   (c) To calculate the cost of the carpet.

David Owen

3   Rather than the calculations referred to in *'Mathematics from 5–16'* (para 4.9), we have in this particular example a most meaningful calculation. However, the shop assistant could not bring his mathematics to bear on an awkward length despite the fact that he had probably been selling carpet for many years. My guess is that when using his calculator the salesman did not know *where to start* (one starting point would be $1 \div 36$ in order to change one inch into a decimal part of a yard. The calculator can then easily handle $5.027 \times 4 \times 9.84 = £197.89$).

An important point for the classroom is that whilst the advent of calculators has made it much less important to be good at arithmetical calculations on paper it has made it much more important (a) to have a firm grasp of mathematical concepts; and (b) to be competent in mental arithmetic.

Mathematical Discussion

Mathematics 5–11, the Cockcroft Report and *Mathematics from 5 to 16* strongly emphasize the importance of discussion in mathematics both between children and between the teacher and children. Once again, some examples for you to consider are given below.

Example A

I was talking to a group of top infants working in a classroom shop when for some bizarre reason it became necessary to subtract 6 from 2. I asked the children, 'What do you think 2 subtract 6 might be?'.

Almost all of them responded very quickly with 'Four!', and then equally quickly with, 'Oh, no it's not, is it!?'. I was just beginning to regret such a barmy question, when one 6-year-old girl saved the situation with the comment, 'I think it's 0, 0, 0, 0, 0'. Perhaps you might think that a silly question deserves a silly answer, but in fact the girl concerned made a huge intellectual jump. She had realized that the set of counting numbers was inadequate in relation to the problem and that it was therefore necessary to invent a new set of numbers. Furthermore (within certain limits) her system works, since

$$2 - 2 = 0$$
$$2 - 3 = 0, 0$$

$2 - 4 = 0, 0, 0$
$2 - 5 = 0, 0, 0, 0$
$2 - 6 = 0, 0, 0, 0, 0$

Implications for the Classroom

1. How can we hope to know anything worth while about the children in our care if we only talk *to* and *at* them? It is also necessary to talk *with* them and this implies, as in the example above, that we listen to children and try to make our own meaning of what they are trying to express. The reward for me in this particular case was that I was there when this little girl invented *her own* mathematics.

2. Assessment and evaluation are popular words in the 1980s. We would do well to remind ourselves that the skilled teacher is constantly assessing children's progress (and his or her own performance as a teacher) through the day-to-day classroom interaction — this is so much richer and more informative than pencil and paper tests and is certainly much better than insulting children by describing them with scores on a standardized test.

> The teacher has to use her judgment continually, making decisions about the need to repeat experiences, to extend them, to consolidate vocabulary, to question or to answer. Conversation — between her and an individual, or a group or the class — is essential as a way of assessing progress and planning the next step. (*Mathematics 5–11*).

Example B

Daniel and Michael, of *The Beano* fame, were attempting to teach themselves to play *Equable* one day. Daniel, who was 7½ at the time, came into my study and said, 'Dad, can you show us how to play *Scrabble*?'.

Like most teachers, I was unable to resist correcting him (!): 'It's not *Scrabble*, Dan, the game is called *Equable* because it's about equations'.

'Oh', he said.

'But, of course, you don't know what an equation is, do you?'.

'No', he said.

David Owen

I wrote 3 + 5 = 8 on a piece of paper and said to him, 'That's a sort of equation'.

'I see', he said.

I then wrote 4 + ☐ = 10.

Dan knew that the unknown number was 6 and so, feeling tempted to do things that I perhaps should not have been doing with a child of that age, I wrote x + 2 = 8 on the paper.

'What's that funny thing?', said Daniel.

'That's an "x". Daddy writes rather funny x's. The x stands for a number that you have to find, just like an empty box can stand for something.'

'I see', he said, and quickly dealt with that one.

I then wrote on the paper 2x + 3 = 11.

'When you are 11 and go to the secondary school, you will have to do equations like this', I said.

'I ought to tell you that 2x means two lots of x — but, of course, you can't do that sort of equation yet'.

'I'm not so sure about that!', Daniel exclaimed, 'can I borrow your pencil?'.

I gave him the pencil and he wrote the following:

4, 5, 6, 7 | 8, 9, 10, 11.

'The answer's 4', he said.

Implications for the Classroom

1 Para 34 of the Cockcroft Report notes that 'most important of all is the need to have sufficient confidence to make effective use of whatever mathematical skill and understanding is possessed whether this be little or much'. Daniel had used his very limited knowledge of mathematics in order to tackle this new problem. It is possible to speculate about the contribution his class teacher may have made. One could suggest the following:
   (a) The child has not been frightened off mathematics. He has no fear about 'having a go'.
   (b) His knowledge might be limited but clearly some very important elements had been dealt with at school (and he was able to bring these to bear on the problem). The elements I have in mind are the ability to:
      — use commutativity (ie $2x + 3 = 3 + 2x$);
      — count on, using a number line (ie from 3 to 11);
      — divide by 2 and know that this is the inverse of doubl-

ing. (I know this because he said to me, 'There are eight jumps from 3 to 11 and that's the same as double the number I don't know.')

2 We may well underestimate children (or overestimate them) if we do not provide them with opportunities to 'talk' mathematics. It is to my shame that I had responded to Daniel's rather cocky manner when dealing with $4 + \square = 10$ and $x + 2 = 8$ by trying to put him down with something he could not do! This is certainly not a technique I would advocate for the classroom and, as you can see, in this particular case I gained my comeuppance!

3 I asked Daniel how he had solved the equation (hence his words quoted in (b) above). I feel that it is very important to provide children with opportunities to describe their methods of tackling particular pieces of work in mathematics. A well-know commercial textbook is often criticized by teachers because it contains such statement as, 'Fred's method', 'Billy's method', 'Susan's method', etc, in relation to particular pieces of mathematics. I would not support these criticisms but my advocation would be that Fred, Billy and Susan should be in *your* class. At times children should be given the opportunity to develop their own ways of tackling a particular piece of mathematics — either individually or, more often, cooperatively. One can speculate on the quality of thinking 11 or 12-year-old, working together, could put to $2x + 3 = 11$ when noting what a 7½-year-old can do. A word of warning, however, for those wanting to try this particular example. It should be noted that this was *not* an example with any degree of reality for Daniel and it certainly did not arise from first-hand experiences. Many teachers will remember their own introduction to algebra as one of the great mysteries of life which they either enjoyed because of its purity or detested because it was totally incomprehensible to them. There are in fact a number of different 'algebras' but the particular algebra used with Daniel is simply generalized arithmetic and can arise powerfully and with meaning from direct experiences or from generalizations arising from children's investigations.

To pursue the point that children should work together and share ideas, I would note that at a very simple (but important) level, children can share ideas about the way they tackle calculations in their heads. For example, to ask a group of fourth year juniors to calculate 102 subtract 68 in their heads and then to tell you how they found the answer is a most useful exercise.

4 In secondary schools, girls generally achieve less well in mathematics than boys, although most primary teachers pride themselves on the fact that there is no noticeable difference at the primary stage. The Assessment of Performance Unit in its 1978[11] and 1979[12] primary surveys found that there were differences between boys and girls on the *type* of mathematics at which they performed well. The complex socialization issues which might be causative are analyzed well within the Cockcroft Report. I raise the matter here because Daniel's willingness to have a go is typical of boys and might well be very significant in relation to problem-solving. The challenge for the primary teacher is to find ways of ensuring that girls are less 'passive and conformist' (in the words of the Cockcroft Report, appendix 2, para B.20) and that their ideas are valued as much as ideas put forward by boys.

Example C

I was visiting a small primary school on the edge of Dartmoor. When I arrived, the headteacher, who had a class of third and fourth year juniors, apologized that she was still finishing a PE session and suggested that I might like to go and look at the pupils' work on display in her room. She suggested that I would find this very interesting but when she added that it was related to a traffic survey my heart sank! There is nothing intrinsically wrong with traffic surveys, it is just that I have seen so many of them. However, when I arrived in her class I saw a magnificent display of children's work, including pictorial representations, art work, and written work. Of particular interest to me was the fact that the pupils had carried out such a wide range of interesting observations. When she arrived back in the class I said to her, 'This is marvellous — how did you get so many ideas!?'. I was really put in my place by her reply, 'I don't get any ideas in this class, Mr Owen, my children are the ideas-people'.

'Come on then, tell me what you did', I said.

'Well, the work actually represents a great deal of cooperation between teachers and children', she replied. 'I couldn't have done it without the support of my supply teacher, but, as I have just said, the real workers were the children. We put the pupils into four groups and asked them to discuss what information they would like to obtain from observing vehicles on the A38 road. They wrote down many possibilities in each group and we assisted them by eliminating those ideas which would be too difficult to carry out. Then, in the same groups, the pupils decided how they were going to collect the information, the observations were made, and finally discussion took place on how to represent the data. We had very much in mind that the audience for the work would be the children in the other classes.'

Implications for the Classroom

Opportunities for children to *work* cooperatively in the classroom must be provided. This example ranged beyond the commonplace since the children's talk was not about work given to them by the teacher. They made a significant contribution to the planning of their own work. Given their heads in this way, the range and quality of the work was very exciting. Although the starting point was mathematical in nature (a survey) it represents a genuine piece of integrated work.

Example D

As a middle infant class was packing up for break, a girl passed me and said, 'I've got cubes in each of these'. She was struggling to carry five plastic food containers, each of which contained some Unifix cubes.

'Are they all the same', I asked, and refined this to, 'are there the same number in each container?' when she hesitated.

'No', she said firmly.

'How could you prove that you are right?', I asked.

By this time we had been joined by a group of six or seven children. Answers poured in:

— 'You could count them.'
— 'No, that would take too long. I would build towers.'
— 'The towers would fall over. I would make trains, but they'd all have to start in the same place.'
— 'I would weigh them all.'

Finally came, 'If I had five jam jars all exactly the same, I would fill each one and see how far the cubes came up the jam jar'.

David Owen

Implications for the Classroom

1 I asked a group of teachers the following day the same question — after ten minutes they managed four approaches to the proof! When I asked the question (of the child) I had only *one* approach in my mind — which might suggest that 6-year-olds think more flexibly than mathematics advisers! Maintaining the interest and enthusiasm for mathematics exhibited by most infants is vital if children are to continue to progress in mathematics.
2 Those who object to my use of the word 'proof' are referred to para 2.32 (Objective 22) in *Mathematics from 5 to 16*, the sentiments of which I entirely share.

Example E

It is appropriate to finish this chapter with a quotation from a paper written by a teacher, Virginia McAnulty, whilst studying for a Primary Mathematics Diploma at the Gwent College of Higher Education:

> One Thursday, in discussion with a group of 5–9-year-olds, they were asked what day it was in Cardiff, a nearby city. Not one child was sure of the answer and discussion continued amongst the children as to whether it was Wednesday or Friday. They were, however, quite sure it was Thursday in Barry Island! Further discussion elicited the fact that all the children had visited Barry Island frequently but few of them had visited Cardiff. Barry Island was within their personal experience, Cardiff was not.

Implications for the Classroom

This example serves to provide us with a final reminder that the child's perception of the world is not always that of the adult. This lack of knowledge about time contrasts strongly with our expectations about children's ability to tell the time from a clock face. As often as possible, the mathematics which the children tackle should find its genesis in first-hand experiences meaningful to them.

The reader is referred to an interesting article in *Mathematics Teaching* by McIntosh entitled 'Some subtractions: What do you think you are doing?'[13]. This reports an exercise where children who were successfully carrying out calculations in subtraction were asked to make up stories and situations to illustrate the computations. Many of their efforts are quite hilarious — if you approve the publication of schoolboy howlers — but tragic if one speculates on the enormous waste of time and effort involved in developing 'subtractors' who do not know when to subtract. To encourage you to refer to the original, I quote just one example here. The child is referring to the calculation 72 subtract 29:

> Paul and Mark went to town. Paul got on the 72 bus and Mark got on the 29 bus and they got off at the 43 bus stop.

In a subsequent piece of work McIntosh discovered that children's grasp of the meaning of multiplication was about as good as their understanding of subtraction.

Notes and References

1 HARDY, GH (1948) *A Mathematician's Apology*, Cambridge, Cambridge University Press.
2 RECORDE, R (1540).
3 COCKCROFT, WH (1982) *Report of the Committee of Enquiry into the Teaching of Mathematics in Schools: Mathematics Counts*, London, HMSO.
4 DEPARTMENT OF EDUCATION AND SCIENCE (1979) *Mathematics 5–11: A Handbook of Suggestions*, London, HMSO.
5 DEPARTMENT OF EDUCATION AND SCIENCE (1985) *Mathematics from 5 to 16*, London, HMSO.
6 AVON LOCAL EDUCATION AUTHORITY (1979) *Maths Extra*, Bristol, Bishopston Teachers Centre.
7 MOTTERSHEAD, L (1978) *Sources of Mathematical Discovery*, Oxford, Basil Blackwell.
8 BOLT, B (1982) *Mathematical Activities*, Cambridge, Cambridge University Press.
9 OPEN UNIVERSITY COURSE (1980) *Mathematics Across the Curriculum No: PME 233*, Milton Keynes, Open University Press.
10 OPEN UNIVERSITY (1980) *Calculators in the Primary School: Student Pack*, Milton Keynes, Open University Press.
11 ASSESSMENT OF PERFORMANCE UNIT (1980) *Mathematical Development. Primary Survey Report No: 1*, London, HMSO.
12 ASSESSMENT OF PERFORMANCE UNIT (1981) *Mathematical Development. Primary Survey Report No: 2*, London, HMSO.
13 MCINTOSH, A (1978) 'Some subtractions: What do you think you are doing?', *Mathematics Teaching*, 83, June.

The Language of Primary Mathematics

Janet Duffin

Introduction

Talking is one of the instruments people use for advancing and developing their thoughts and ideas. Listening is one of the instruments people use to help them grasp other people's ideas and thoughts. Discussion takes place among two or more people when both talking and listening occur and when there is a genuine desire on the part of all participants to further mutual understanding in order to extend the thinking of all.

Much has been written about the place of discussion, talking, and the sharing of ideas and meaning in language development in schools and there can be few primary teachers unaware of its importance in their classrooms. What may be slightly less well understood by primary teachers is the place and function of discussion in the mathematics lesson. This is not to say that language has not featured in mathematics lessons — indeed there are forms of words which can be found in use in mathematics lessons in countries as far apart as England, Australia and Africa, but these have all tended to be set phrases associated with processes, usually presented as pencil and paper techniques and practised endlessly to achieve what it is hoped will be a lifelong proficiency. These have often had nothing whatever to do with either language or mathematical development in any true sense of those words.

Sometimes these forms of words do not bear examination when their meaning is considered and it can be shown not only that they are being used incorrectly in terms of their linguistic sense but that, in addition, they obscure the mathematics they are intended to facilitate. The word 'borrow' in the subtraction process is an obvious example and many teachers have now realized, through the use of structual apparatus to help children with this process, that it is an inappropriate word and have begun to adopt other words which relate more closely to the activity involved when the apparatus is used. This is an important development in the mathematics classroom for it shows, in a way that is already familiar to many teachers, that language arising from an activity is more useful and helpful to children in their mathematical development than a form of words introduced by the teacher to 'help' them to 'remember what to do'.

The rapid and far-reaching changes that have occurred in language development in the primary school since the Bullock Report[1] of 1975 now have to be looked at in the context of mathematics, both because the corresponding report in mathematics, the Cockcroft Report of 1982[2], drew attention to the importance of language in mathematical development, and because many teachers and others working in mathematical education had begun to realize the same thing.

Language Development

It is appropriate, therefore, to mention briefly the work of those involved in language development which has influenced the thought of those concerned with mathematical education. In language development a great deal of stress is laid on the need to have something of interest to talk about, of the importance of a 'shared meaning' between the speaker and the listener. Shared meanings help to ensure that communication takes place. They are also appropriate for talk in the mathematics lesson. Moreover, it has been established that in learning to read children have less difficulty with words which are already part of their spoken vocabulary. This too has some pertinent implications for the mathematics lesson as I shall try to indicate later.

Barbara Tizard and Martin Hughes, in their book *Young Children Learning*[3], make similar points about the importance of talk to the learning process. They suggest that in the home where children talk with their parents about activities undertaken together, often initiated by the child, the child's level of thinking can be at a higher level than that often observed in nursery schools. How often must primary teachers have observed and listened to the chatter of children in the playground or dining room and yet have been confronted with children who become tongue-tied when asked a question in a mathematics lesson. If this is the case what can be done to improve the situation so that children become more mathematically articulate?

The Wider Context

The answer to this question lies, at least in part, with the fact that to many people mathematics is frightening and its mathematical language, except where it is also part of everyday language, is unlikly to feature much in everyday speech. Moreover, it is unlikely to become part of the natural spoken language of children in the home. Indeed, in a survey of the spoken vocabulary of 8-year-olds in America[4], only about 10 per cent of a list of 3000 words familiar to the children were associated with the processes and concepts of mathematics, and only about 1 or 2 per cent were words from the genuine language of mathematicians. Of these last, most indeed were words which would have been encountered in non-mathematical situations and have meanings quite distinct from their mathematical ones. Examples such as ring, group and neighbourhood, indeed, are words which are unlikely to be known in a mathematical sense to more than a handful of adults, whereas map, set and match will occur fairly early in a child's school experience but may not be known in a mathematical context to their parents and other adults with whom they talk outside school.

If we develop this idea a little further by looking at reading tests designed to establish a child's reading age we notice, both in the simple word recognition tests (such as Burt and Schonell) and in the more comprehensive test (such as Holborn and others) that, in the main, few mathematical words or situations are included. This reinforces the view that mathematical language does not feature much in either the spoken or written language used to test language development generally.

Developing Language in Mathematics Teaching

Some children were collecting starfish in a rockpool. They counted their finds and had reached 94: 'We need six more ... now we have 97, three more' they said as they filled the pool. Would those same children have been able to operate so slickly if they had been asked to subtract 94 or 97 from 100 in sum form:

The Language of Primary Mathematics

$$100 - 94 \quad \text{or} \quad \begin{array}{r} 100 \\ -\ 97 \\ \hline \end{array}$$

or even in word form: how many more do you need to make up 100 if you already have 94?

If we begin to listen to children and to share in their experiences through talking with them we can be surprised and delighted at the level of mathematical thought that they can demonstrate. Examples include:

(a) a 3-year-old who thought about two ninety-nines and arrived without difficulty at 198;
(b) a 4-year-old who talked about sharing numbers and non-sharing numbers;
(c) a 5-year-old who, on misdealing some cards so that they were in two piles of seventeen and nineteen, said, after initially thinking that two must be taken from the nineteen pile, 'No, if I give you one we'll both have eighteen'.

A situation similar to the last of these occurred in a primary classroom where a teacher was sorting with a group of children and two sets had been identified: a set of cylinders and a set of red assorted shapes. Thinking to introduce a little number work into the activity, the teacher drew the children's attention to the fact that one set contained five objects and the other nine. 'How could we balance them?' she said. Several different answers came, and teacher and class settled for the one which entailed removing four of the red shapes so that there were two sets containing five objects. In the activity there was some nice use of language: more than, less than and matching, but one child, at the stage when suggestions were being made and evaluated, volunteered: 'They would balance if we took two from the red set and put them with the cylinders'. Because this would have upset the sets by introducing red shapes into the set of cylinders, the answer was not accepted and yet ... the child, concentrating on the idea of balance and disregarding the original sets, had shown a level of thought which was higher than that of merely taking away four objects from a set of nine objects. This answer the teacher disregarded.

How often in the classroom do teachers ask a question with a 'correct' answer in mind which causes them to reject an answer from a child which does not accord with a 'correct' answer? There must be few teachers who could say that they have never been guilty of such a practice. Indeed, Brissenden[5], who has worked on the development of mathematical talk with children in Swansea, observed what he calls the three-term sequence in mathematics teaching.

The teacher asks a question, the child replies, the teacher evaluates the child's answer frequently rejecting it, while the child continues to find the 'right' answer. This process of evaluation argues Brissenden inhibits real discussion because the children are trying to find the answer that will satisfy the teacher instead of giving free rein to their own interpretation of what was asked. Teachers would do better to ask questions without immediately seeking a correct answer. In this way children are freer to express themselves and the teacher can concentrate on listening to the children in order to find out how they are thinking. This way the teacher not only finds out how the children are thinking but also whether his questions have been interpreted in the way he expected. In this way both the learning and the teaching process may be improved. In fact the Primary Language Group of the Mathematical Association summed this up by saying, 'It may be more important for the teacher to understand what the pupil says than for the pupil to understand what the teacher says[6]', though clearly both are important.

This idea has also been echoed by mathematical educators in one way or another from many parts of the world[7]:

(a) language plays an increasingly important role in mathematics as children move through the system;
(b) if children cannot talk with their teacher and each other they cannot make progress in mathematics;
(c) mathematics must be more verbal; we can learn a lot by listening to children.

A Summary So Far

The following have been touched on so far:

(i) Discussion is an important way to develop thought.
(ii) Language development may be as important in mathematics as in other areas of the curriculum.
(iii) Acquisition of spoken mathematical vocabulary may be useful in helping to read mathematical texts.
(iv) Much mathematical language does not feature in the natural language of many people.
(v) Language coming out of activity provides a better way to

The Language of Primary Mathematics

        develop mathematically than language built on to a mathematical process.
- (vi) Mathematics based on reality has more meaning for children than calculations presented out of context.
- (vii) Teachers need to listen to what children actually say rather than concentrating on their own perception of the correct answer to a question they have asked.

Now is a need to understand language in practice in the mathematics education of young children.

Talk and Thought in Practice

The question to be answered is, 'How can we begin to build into the mathematics lesson the kind of conditions which occur naturally in the home so that the thinking abilities of children can be extended through language in mathematics lessons and avoid those conditions which in inhibit talk and stultify thought?'.

    One person who has worked on this idea for a number of years is Zoe Evans in Exeter. She came to teaching with a fear of mathematics which she did not wish to communicate to the children she was to teach. She was given a brief by her headteacher to organize early work for infants which would develop them mathematically but she was to do this without recorded 'sums'. Zoe believed that mathematics should be unthreatening and she set to work to devise materials for her classroom which would be both demanding mathematically and at the same time familiar to the children. She based her materials on sets and sorting, with number concepts embedded in them, and she used bags of 'toys', specially created to develop concepts of weight, size, colour, etc and made in materials which were visually and tactually pleasing to the children. She wove stories round the toys and her children gained powers of discrimination which were occasionally almost too refined. The children enjoyed their mathematics lessons so much that she was able to use the device 'If you're naughty I won't let you do your maths'. Some of Zoe's materials are now available for purchase to make up[8]. She calls her approach Experience into Language into Mathematics.

    Many teachers may not feel they can go to the lengths of buying and making up the many sets used by Zoe in her work and they will need to look around them to find other suitable materials and activities which can be used to generate talk. These abound: bottle tops, counters, pegs, cubes etc, which can be used to generate number shapes and from these number facts such as factors, fractions, square numbers. Wheel hubs, manholes, windows, doors, and those plastic tops you can put on your drink to take on a train, can show properties of symmetry, and there are many other examples.

There is a delightful video from the Open University[9] which shows children finding fractions of twenty-four using bottle tops. From their discussion it is clear that even though they 'know their tables', the facts within those tables only become clear to them when they play with the bottle tops. It is the case that children's perceptions of something may differ markedly from that of their teacher. In her book *Children's Minds*[10], Margaret Donaldson explores ways in which children may appear to be showing a lack of understanding of a mathematical idea which, on further examination, can be seen to be because of their differing perception of a situation, sometimes because of words which sound the same but mean something different, such as hare and hair. It is most important that teachers realize that these differences may arise at any time in any classroom setting. This makes it all the more important for the teacher to listen to children so that these differing perceptions can be identified and if necessary, corrected. When teachers and children listen to each other it is possible for the children to become precise in their use of mathematical terms and forms of words in a way that is difficult if not impossible in some more formal classrooms.

For many teachers it is a difficult exercise to learn to listen to children. Most of us know the value of teaching through asking questions and most of us become quite skilled in the art of questioning as a teaching tool. Unfortunately most of these questions are of the 'I have the right answer in my mind' variety and this does not fit with the concept of genuine discussion which presupposes that the understanding of all, not just that of the pupil, will be developed by the discussion. Brissenden, in his book *Teaching Mathematics — Theory into Practice*[11] has some helpful suggestions for teachers who wish to change their teaching style from a prescriptive to a more open-ended one.

The Same and Different

In order to clarify some aspects of language which might be helpful to teachers it may be useful to consider the implications for the classroom of the fact that there are words which have different meanings in mathematics from their meaning in ordinary everyday language. In order that teachers may be on the alert for difficulties arising in the classroom because of this it would be helpful for them to have developed a classification of words for the mathematics lesson into (i) those which occur in both everyday speech and in mathematics; (ii) those which have different meanings in everyday speech from their meaning in mathematics; and (iii) those words which only occur in a mathematical context. For those which occur only in a mathematical context it would be necessary to try to devise interesting and appropriate activities which could be used as a setting for their introduction.

Another way to think about language for the classroom is to classify one's teaching vocabulary into:

(a) those words which are specific to mathematical language;
(b) those words which are highly associated with mathematical concepts and processes such as prepositions of position, of measurement etc, as well as verbs, adjectives and nouns associated with processes (even, odd, add, subtract, pentagon and all the shape names and properties);
(c) those words which might arise from classroom activities devised to generate mathematics.

The last of these, though it is about words which are not themselves directly mathematical, relates to the ability to be aware of the mathematical potential of many classroom activities, besides seeing how activities specific to other aspects of the curriculum often also have mathematical potential.

Let us pause again to summarize what has been said in the second part of this chapter:

(i) Making mathematics unthreatening and related to children's own interests.
(ii) Using talk to develop mathematical language, extend perceptions.
(iii) Being aware of different meanings of words in mathematics and ordinary speech.
(iv) Experience into Language into Mathematics — unthreatening material.
(v) Different ways to classify language.
(vi) Seeing the mathematical potential in activities in other subject areas.

Janet Duffin

Implicit in all that has been said so far is the idea that we are trying to move away from the idea of mathematics at the primary level as being about the acquisition of the basic skills of number through pencil and paper calculations. This is so not only because the arrival of a new technology totally undermines the needs of the last century for efficient and universally used written methods and of calculation but also because it is now recognized that it is essential for the mathematical development of the child that both practical and oral elements, as well as the manipulation on paper of mathematical symbols and formulae, must play a part. Electronic calculators are becoming the new computation aid as well as being seen as a way of generating mathematics and helping children to learn how to cope with the problem-solving and investigations that are coming into the mathematics curriculum. And teachers are now finding out that all these new devices and processes are more effective in developing mathematics if they include talk. In order to be able to solve problems children need to be able to explain what they are doing; in order to demonstrate a process on a calculator it is useful to be able to communicate this orally and thereby to understand and explain it. It is increasingly evident that in order to become articulate mathematically, children must practise talking in all their mathematics lessons.

In Contrast

Let us take an example of a traditional classroom where children are working on a well-known scheme; doing a page of examples, getting their work marked, seeing the teacher entering their results on an assessment sheet. One child had completed the following problem:

> Eggs are packed in boxes of six. How many boxes are needed for 8000 eggs?

The child had done this as follows and it had been marked wrong:

$$6 \overline{)8000} = 1333 \text{ r}2$$

The teacher was asked what he did in this case. He replied that the child was showing that he was not ready for the psychological jump necessary to get back from the sum to the real solution to the problem. Asked what he did about it he replied that he just says to the child 'How many boxes are needed?'. If the child cannot then see the answer he or she is not ready to see it.

The teacher seemed to be seeing maturation as a natural process not to be interfered with. But is is not. It can be helped along with talk. Like this:

> Here we have 8000 eggs. How many boxes are we going to need? Can you think of any number of boxes we would certainly need? And I (the teacher) might be hoping the child would volunteer a number such as, perhaps, that 1000 boxes would do for 6000 eggs. The discussion might then proceed to how many eggs would still be left without boxes and then to go on to see how many eggs could be boxed next. With 2000 eggs left there are various possibilities available to proceed to. A bright child might see that 300 boxes would deal with 1800 eggs leaving 200 to be boxed, followed by thirty boxes for 180 eggs leaving twenty still to be boxed. This way, when the final two eggs remain, the need for a box for them might emerge without further difficulty.

Of course all this might not be achieved without any recording at all, but the kind of recording would not be related to a specific method of setting down and would come instead from a need to keep in mind what had been happening.

> For instance, 6000 eggs into 1000 boxes
> 2000 eggs left
> 1800 eggs into 300 boxes leaving 200 eggs
> 180 eggs into thirty boxes leaving twenty eggs
> 18 eggs into three boxes leaving two eggs,

or more formally:

$$
\begin{array}{rl}
8000 & \\
\underline{6000} & 6 \times 1000 \\
2000 & \\
\underline{1800} & 6 \times 300 \\
200 & \\
\underline{180} & 6 \times 30 \\
20 & \\
\underline{18} & 6 \times 3 \\
2 &
\end{array}
$$

But we need a box for the last two eggs so 1334 boxes are needed altogether.

This way, the recording would relate to the activity and the second version is a formalization which is helpful for recalling the activity and the thought processes used. This is conjectural since it did not happen. Here is an example that did.

The problem was to find how far a cyclist would go in five minutes if he can go 2 km in eight minutes. The child was trying to reconcile his recorded work with his own intuitive perception of the problem. He said that 2 km in eight minutes meant 1 km in four minutes. He then volunteered that in five minutes the distance would be one and a quarter kilometres but he was puzzled by what he himself had written down. He was appalled by his own work:

$$2\overline{)8}^{4} \qquad\qquad \begin{array}{r} 4\times \\ \underline{5} \\ 20 \end{array}$$

He studied what he had written and then suddenly said 'Oh, it's two-eighths' following that with 'If I write down $8\overline{)2}$ the answer is remainder 2'. He then wrote down

$$\begin{array}{r} 25\times \\ \underline{5} \\ 125 \end{array}$$

At this point the bell went and he had to stop — bells are important in that school! It seemed to me that in arriving at 125 the child was almost there. He had not been using stylized thought, either then or when he had earlier volunteered the correct answer with no explanation, but he still seemed to be tied to stylized recording which somehow obscured his own thought processes.

Here was a child who could think but because of being tied to the standard ways of recording mathematics he had been unable to articulate and then record his actual thought processes. He could clearly think mathematically and, given the opportunity to verbalize and record his own thoughts in the form in which he thought them, I believe he might have come to a better understanding and eventually also a better performance.

Unnecessary Obstacles

In the same class a child had her hand up. I went to her and asked her what her problem was. 'No problem' she said, 'but I've finished the page and I have to have them marked now'. I asked if she knew how she could check her own work so that she wouldn't need to have it marked. She said no. We looked at her 'sums'.

The Language of Primary Mathematics

$$\begin{array}{r}26\\4\overline{)104}\end{array}$$

I showed her that if she multiplied the 4 and the 26 she could check that she was correct by seeing if the result was 104. It was. She was very pleased and set about checking all her own answers instead of sitting with her hand up. When we left the classroom at the end of the lesson she caught up with me and said 'Your method doesn't always work'. 'Doesn't it?' I said, 'let's see.' She showed me

$$\begin{array}{r}15\ r6\\8\overline{)126}\end{array}$$

'It doesn't work' she said 'because 8 times 15 is 120 not 126.' '120' I said 'and how many more are there?' 'Oh of course, that's the remainder 6'.

In that class the children were multiplying and dividing by ten thus:

$$\begin{array}{r}42\ r8\\10\overline{)428}\end{array} \qquad \begin{array}{r}213\times\\10\\\hline 2130\end{array}$$

and saying as they did so

10 into 4 won't go carry 4, 10 into 42 goes 4 r2 10 into 28 goes 2 r8

Ten 3s are 30, put down 0 and carry 3, ten 1s are 10 and 3 makes 13, put down 3 and carry 1 ten 2s are 20 and 1 is 21.

The above demonstrates how well those children had been taught the verbal steps and phrases to carry out the multiplication and division processes as recorded calculations, but they in no way showed signs of recognizing mathematical principles, or that such calculations could be carried out easily in the head, and the processes recorded or spoken in words.

Encouraged earlier to verbalize their mathematical processes, those children might instead have been saying something like:

For the division:
There are 40 tens in 400, there are 2 tens in 20, so the answer is 42 with 8 remainder.

For the multiplication:
Multiplication by 10 moves the figures one place to the left so the answer is 2130 because I have to put a 0 to show the figures have moved.

Janet Duffin

or if they were older:
When I divide by 10 the figures
move one place to the right so
the answer is 42.8.

Armed with that kind of ability to verbalize and justify and check their calculations, these children and others might be on the way towards being able to take both an oral and a practical examination in the new GCSE. Without practice of the kind suggested, from the earliest stages, when they might be asked say to tell a story about six or to say as many things about six as they could, these children will not be in a position to pass the new examinations.

So once again the responsibility of the primary schools is to lay the foundations for later work, building on the clear evidence that pre-school children can think mathematically provided they are presented with real situations to which they can relate.

Formalized recording is unnecessary to with very young children, as is the use of mathematical symbols. What is essential is to concentrate on developing mathematical thought and the ability to articulate that thought. Ruth a child of 3, counts objects confidently and correctly to five. Her mother says she can do it to fifteen but when presented with numerals the child could not name any of them. How much better to build on what the child can do, and extend her thought and her language, than start her on the way to the sums her older sister may be doing without mathematical understanding at her school.

Notes and References

1. DEPARTMENT OF EDUCATION AND SCIENCE (1975) *A Language for Life* (The Bullock Report), London, HMSO.
2. COCKCROFT, WH (1982) *Report of the Committee of Enquiry into the Teaching of Mathematics in Schools: Mathematics Counts*, London, HMSO.
3. TIZARD, B and HUGHES, H (1984) *Young Children Learning*, London, Fontana.
4. Dale word lists of spoken vocabulary of American 8-year-olds.
5. BRISSENDEN, TF (1982) 'Rewriting the mathematics script', *Mathematics in School*, 14, 4.
6. MATHEMATICAL ASSOCIATION (1983) *Primary Language Group, Maths Round the Country*, Leicester, Mathematical Association.
7. Annual conference of the Psychology of Mathematics Education Group: quotes from various international speakers.

The Language of Primary Mathematics

$$\frac{26}{4\overline{)104}}$$

I showed her that if she multiplied the 4 and the 26 she could check that she was correct by seeing if the result was 104. It was. She was very pleased and set about checking all her own answers instead of sitting with her hand up. When we left the classroom at the end of the lesson she caught up with me and said 'Your method doesn't always work'. 'Doesn't it?' I said, 'let's see.' She showed me

$$\frac{15 \text{ r}6}{8\overline{)126}}$$

'It doesn't work' she said 'because 8 times 15 is 120 not 126.' '120' I said 'and how many more are there?' 'Oh of course, that's the remainder 6'.

In that class the children were multiplying and dividing by ten thus:

$$\frac{42 \text{ r}8}{10\overline{)428}} \qquad\qquad \begin{array}{r} 213\times \\ 10 \\ \hline 2130 \end{array}$$

and saying as they did so

10 into 4 won't go carry 4, 10 into 42 goes 4 r2 10 into 28 goes 2 r8	Ten 3s are 30, put down 0 and carry 3, ten 1s are 10 and 3 makes 13, put down 3 and carry 1 ten 2s are 20 and 1 is 21.

The above demonstrates how well those children had been taught the verbal steps and phrases to carry out the multiplication and division processes as recorded calculations, but they in no way showed signs of recognizing mathematical principles, or that such calculations could be carried out easily in the head, and the processes recorded or spoken in words.

Encouraged earlier to verbalize their mathematical processes, those children might instead have been saying something like:

For the division:
There are 40 tens in 400, there are 2 tens in 20, so the answer is 42 with 8 remainder.

For the multiplication:
Multiplication by 10 moves the figures one place to the left so the answer is 2130 because I have to put a 0 to show the figures have moved.

or if they were older:
When I divide by 10 the figures
move one place to the right so
the answer is 42.8.

Armed with that kind of ability to verbalize and justify and check their calculations, these children and others might be on the way towards being able to take both an oral and a practical examination in the new GCSE. Without practice of the kind suggested, from the earliest stages, when they might be asked say to tell a story about six or to say as many things about six as they could, these children will not be in a position to pass the new examinations.

So once again the responsibility of the primary schools is to lay the foundations for later work, building on the clear evidence that pre-school children can think mathematically provided they are presented with real situations to which they can relate.

Formalized recording is unnecessary to with very young children, as is the use of mathematical symbols. What is essential is to concentrate on developing mathematical thought and the ability to articulate that thought. Ruth a child of 3, counts objects confidently and correctly to five. Her mother says she can do it to fifteen but when presented with numerals the child could not name any of them. How much better to build on what the child can do, and extend her thought and her language, than start her on the way to the sums her older sister may be doing without mathematical understanding at her school.

Notes and References

1 DEPARTMENT OF EDUCATION AND SCIENCE (1975) *A Language for Life* (The Bullock Report), London, HMSO.
2 COCKCROFT, WH (1982) *Report of the Committee of Enquiry into the Teaching of Mathematics in Schools: Mathematics Counts*, London, HMSO.
3 TIZARD, B and HUGHES, H (1984) *Young Children Learning*, London, Fontana.
4 Dale word lists of spoken vocabulary of American 8-year-olds.
5 BRISSENDEN, TF (1982) 'Rewriting the mathematics script', *Mathematics in School*, 14, 4.
6 MATHEMATICAL ASSOCIATION (1983) *Primary Language Group, Maths Round the Country*, Leicester, Mathematical Association.
7 Annual conference of the Psychology of Mathematics Education Group: quotes from various international speakers.

8 EVANS, Z (1985) *Snakes without Ladders*, London, Hendre Centre.
9 OPEN UNIVERSITY (1980) *Developing Mathematical Thinking*, Milton Keynes, Open University.
10 DONALDSON, M (1978) *Children's Minds*, London, Fontana.
11 BRISSENDEN, TF (1980) *Teaching Mathematics — Theory into Practice*, London, Harper and Row.

Mathematics Across the Curriculum

Alan Sutcliffe

Mathematics at Large

The mathematical needs of the whole curriculum provide excellent opportunities for placing mathematics in context. Where the use of class teachers is the norm, as in primary schools, it is the responsibility of each individual teacher to ensure that mathematics is used where appropriate opportunities occur.[1]

The aim of this chapter is to highlight, with examples, the different types of opportunities which might be used by primary school teachers to place mathematics in context in other areas of the curriculum.

In nursery classes children are not taught in terms of the traditional subject areas. At this level teaching is normally incidental and proceeds naturally from the situations in which the children are involved.

The approach used by good nursery teachers is well outlined in the Schools Council Publication *Early Mathematical Experiences*.[2] For example, a nursery teacher observing children playing on a see-saw would naturally consider whether this was an appropriate opportunity to discuss with the children involved ideas linked with the concept of mass such as 'up, down, heavier than, lighter than, weighs more than, weighs less than, balances, weighs the same as ...'.

From the children's responses in such play situations the experienced teacher is able to judge the level of the children's thinking and to consider the stage which their conceptual development has reached. She might also consider in which situations opportunities for the development of subsequent stages in the concept of mass may occur. For instance, whilst children are playing in the sand tray. It is through experiences in a variety of such contexts that conceptual understanding is most effectively developed.

Difficulties associated with the assessment and recording of children's learning within such incidental situations are not understimated. Readers who have not already done so may wish to consider the approach to this problem suggested by Julia Matthews.[3]

As children move up the primary school the same situations may be used at increasingly sophisticated levels of mathematical development. For instance, the activity of cooking can at first involve measuring skills associated with non-standard units of capacity (cupful, spoonful ...). At a subsequent stage standard units of capacity may be used (litres, millilitres, ...). In both cases skills of estimation and approximation will be involved.

Children need to practice such skills regularly if they are to achieve fluency but the practice should be embedded in the relevant conceptual structures and where possible experienced in appropriate practical situations in other curriculum areas. The children will then be able to perceive the purpose behind the use of such skills.

In contrast to this approach the tendency in some commercial mathematics schemes is to regard measurement skills as ends in themselves and to provide practice in artificial situations which are unrelated to purposeful activities.

Understanding and Context

> Conceptual understanding is most effectively developed through the use of mathematics in a variety of contexts ... the context might be any need perceived by the pupils: ... work in another subject in the curriculum or a topic of interest.[4]

In many infant classes it is common practice for children to learn through the medium of a topic or centre of interest. Sometimes the full mathematical significance of such topics is not always realized.

The children should be challenged to explore new ideas and to devise their own methods for the solution of problems relevant to the topic.

The following sections analyze the mathematical significance of some experiences associated with a topic on 'People who help us: the postman' at infant level and a project on orienteering with juniors. The analyses will be in terms of facts, skills, conceptual structures and general strategies.

Enhancing Skills

Research shows that these three elements — facts and skills, conceptual structures, general strategies and appreciation — involve distinct aspects of teaching and require separate attention. It follows that effective mathematics teaching must pay attention to all three.[5]

Skills refer to the children's practical ability to perform a task. They involve procedures which often include the use of a routine. For instance in writing the numeral 5 it is normal to proceed as shown below:

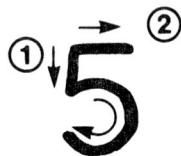

Skills need to be practised and can often be related to a conceptual structure in which they should be embedded. Here the ability to write the numeral 5 needs to be related to the concept of five as a cardinal number and as an ordinal number lying between 4 and 6 in the set of natural numbers.

This is an example of a conceptual structure. Such rich inter-connections should, where possible, underpin the performance of skills. Their presence can often help children to remedy a memory failure or enable them to adapt a procedure to a new, but similar, situation.

By general strategies we mean those abilities which help us to choose which skills to use in order to solve a particular problem. For a full discussion of these terms, and useful examples of each, readers are referred to ATM.[6]

A real-life problem situation could be set up by giving each infant in a group an envelope with a street name written upon it. The children can then be asked to complete the address on their envelope by adding a numeral. Depending upon the age, ability and experience of the group it may be necessary to restrict the set of numerals to be used (say to twenty or less). The addresses may then be read out by the children and the envelopes collected and displayed.

Discussion can then range round the 'best' way of collecting up

Mathematics Across the Curriculum

the envelopes ready for delivery to the 'houses' on the particular street.

The concepts and skills involved will be concerned with odd and even numbers, sequences of numbers and the matching of envelopes to houses. Strategies for 'delivery' will need to consider the time and distance necessary to cover different routes in zig-zag or rectangular formations.

This approach to one particularly mathematical aspect of a topic will help children to appreciate that mathematics helps us to solve such real-life problems involving distance and time. A similar appreciation has been observed in a group of junior school children who worked for a term on the mathematics involved in the sport of orienteering.

This sport normally involves finding particular points (known as controls) in a forest environment using a specially prepared map. Permanent orienteering courses are now to be found in many areas of the country and details of these may be obtained from the British Orienteering Foundation.[7] However, experience with junior school children has led one to realize that the principles and procedures of this sport can be simplified and used in any school which has a reasonably sized playground or adjacent sports field.

The chart shows an analysis of the mathematics involved in orienteering in terms of facts, skills, concepts and strategies.

Facts are essentially arbitrary pieces of information which the children will need to be told since they are unlikely to be able to discover them for themselves. It is a fact that the red end of a SILVA compass[8] normally points to the north. It is a fact that grid references are conventionally given with the set of numbers representing the W–E position before that set which respresents the S–N position.

A spring term project with a J3 and J4 class required about three hours of work each week. This was in addition to the normal daily mathematics lessons. Though the more difficult concepts of scale and contours were not reached the children were involved in a great deal of mathematical experience and motivation was high. The pupils did not appear to realize that they were doing mathematics during their 'maps' project.

The children were first asked to draw a map which would guide some long lost relatives to their homes. The constraint that the map should fit on one piece of A4 would have prevented some children (who perhaps did not have an intuitive feeling for scale) from using several A4 sheets for their maps!

Alan Sutcliffe

Figure 1

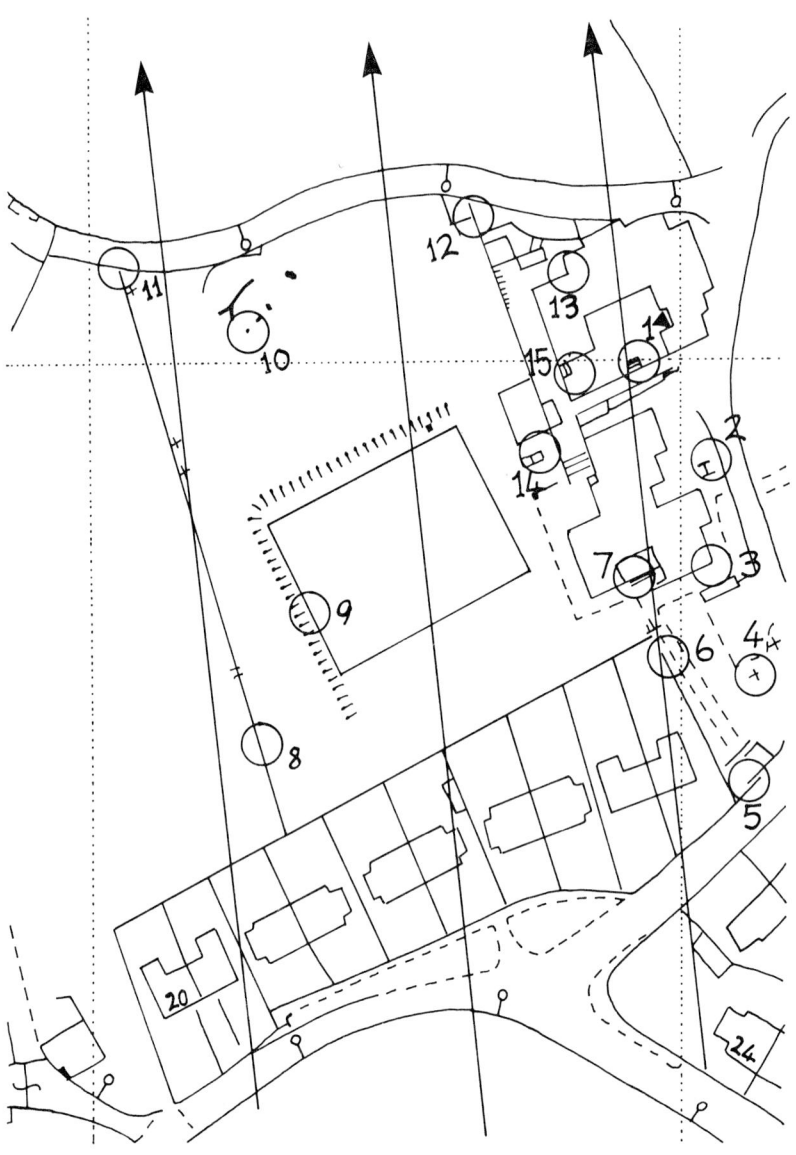

Figure 2

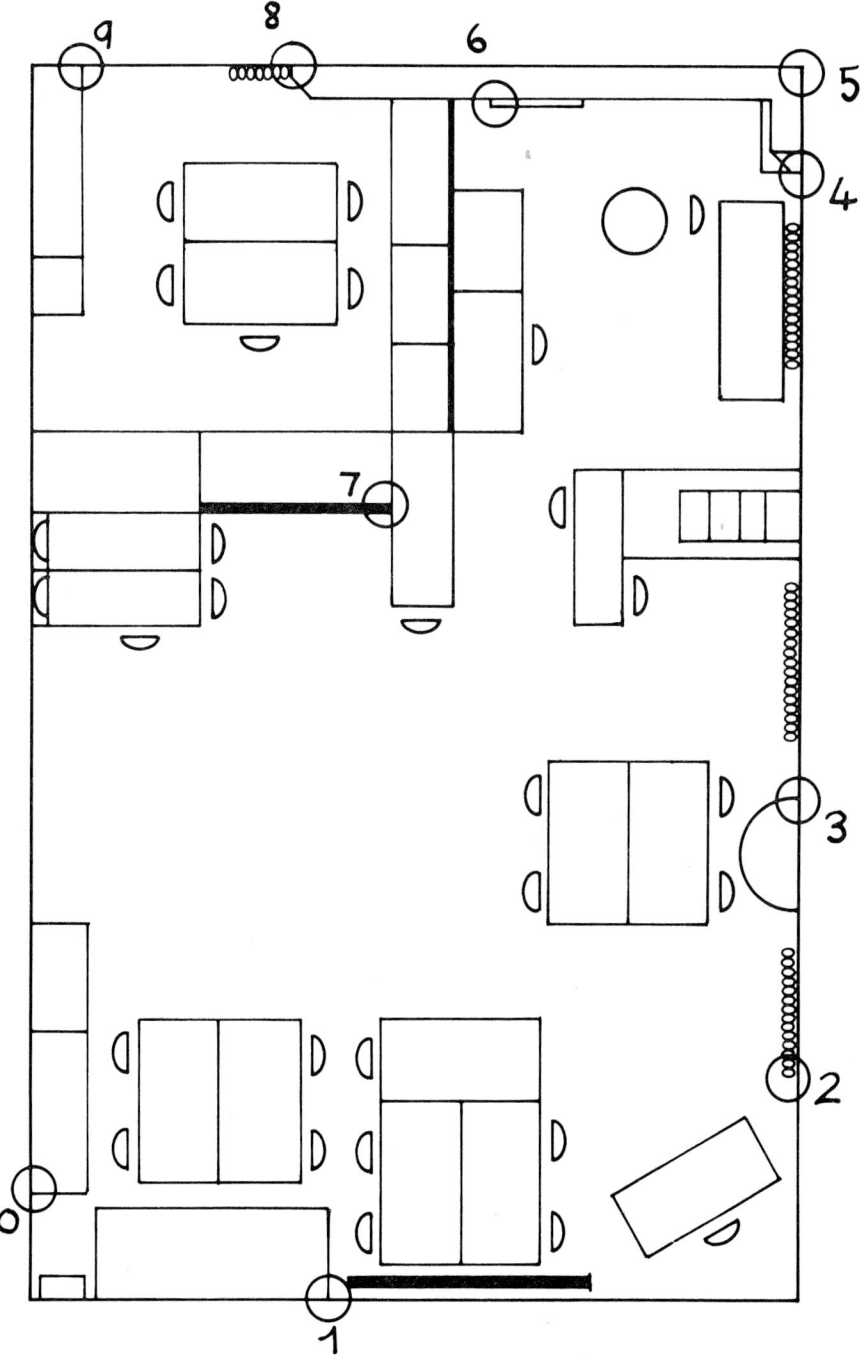

Alan Sutcliffe

Next, maps of the classroom were drawn and the best map was reproduced. These maps were then available to the children as an on-going classroom orienteering exercise to gainfully occupy early finishers during the term.[9] The exercise involved the important skills of orienting the map so that it matched the classroom and of relating positions on the map to the corresponding positions in the classroom.

Which direction? *Finding the place*

Walking on a bearing (skill)
Orienting the map (skill) Grid references (fact, skill)
Magnetic North (fact) Symbols from legend (facts)

Orienteering

How far? *Route choice* (strategy)

Pace counting (skill) Contours (concept)
Distance (concept) Contour interval (concept)
Scale (concept) Gradient (concept)

It will be clear from the network model that some of the mathematical skills and concepts involved in orienteering are at an advanced level.

Walking on a bearing, for instance, involves being able to set a bearing on the compass (one graduation on the dial usually represents two degrees), face in the correct direction and then walk in that direction after lining up an object in the distance with the compass needle. The skill of setting a bearing should be embedded in the conceptual structure of angle as an amount of turn which should have been built up over the years using a spiral approach.

Children can be told that 1cm on a map of scale 1:10000 (a frequently used orienteering scale) represents 100m on the ground. However, the ability to deal with scale, at anything other than a rote level, will depend upon the children's experience of the related conceptual structures.

And More Practice

Thus, even with upper junior children, a great deal of related practical experience may need to be given before they can deal with problems of scale with understanding. Three-dimensional shapes

Figure 3:

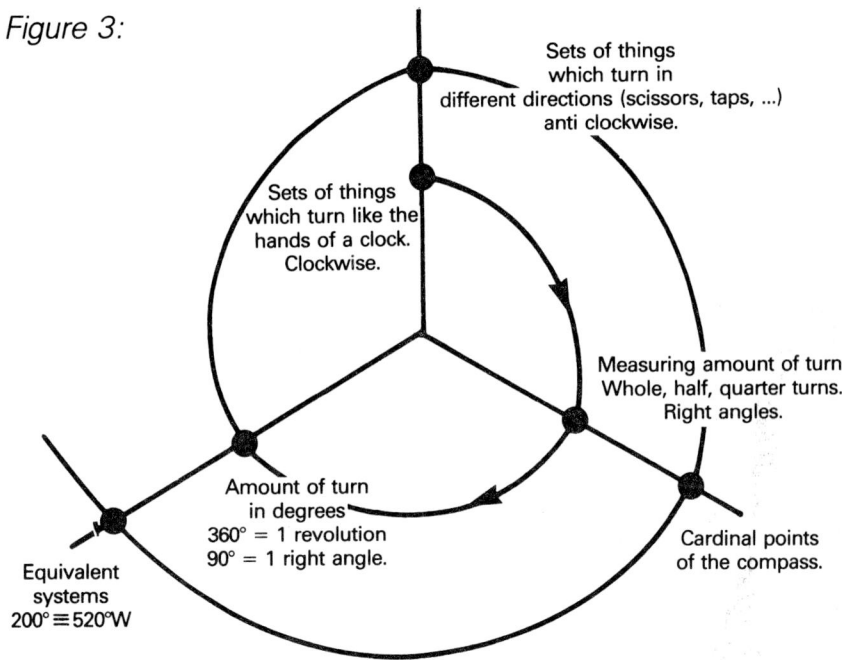

should be enlarged. Cubes, then cuboids and finally simple models, may be enlarged so that shape is maintained through size increases. Moving to two-dimensional the same procedure may be followed using sticky paper squares, equilateral triangles and rectangles. Whilst most children will deal with the enlargement of shapes using cubes and squares, cuboids and rectangles will be more difficult for them. Many children will increase the size of the shape in two or one dimensions, only rather than the three or two dimensions which are necessary. Shapes may also be enlarged, or reduced, by using squared paper of different sizes. Finally simple plans may be drawn using a scale of 1:2. Difficulties associated with measuring may be overcome, if necessary, by using strips of paper which can then be folded the desired number of times.

Thus, before a teacher can deal effectively with the application of mathematics to a sport like orienteering she should have available in her mind the mathematics involved as a set of related conceptual structures. This will enable her to decide upon the route to be taken through the concepts in the particular context, such as orienteering, which interests her. The teacher will be proceeding from the curriculum context to the mathematics. The children will be well motivated because they can appreciate the purpose and the application of the concepts which they are studying.

Alan Sutcliffe

Enlarging Shapes.

1. Use the squares to make two more squares which have:
   (a) sides twice as long,
   (b) sides three times as long.

2. Now use the equilateral triangles to make two more triangles which have the same shape but with sides:
   (a) twice as long
   (b) three times as long.

3. Repeat number two but this time use the rectangles.

4. What do you notice about the number of shapes you needed?

5. Use your shapes to make a picture. Now make the same picture but with sides twice as long.

6. Write about your picture.

Mathematics Across the Curriculum

1a)

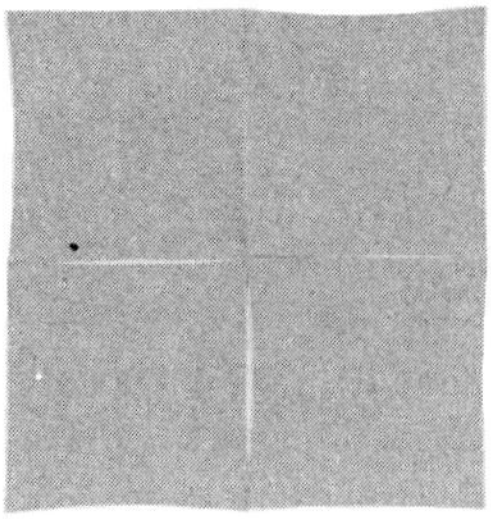

1b)

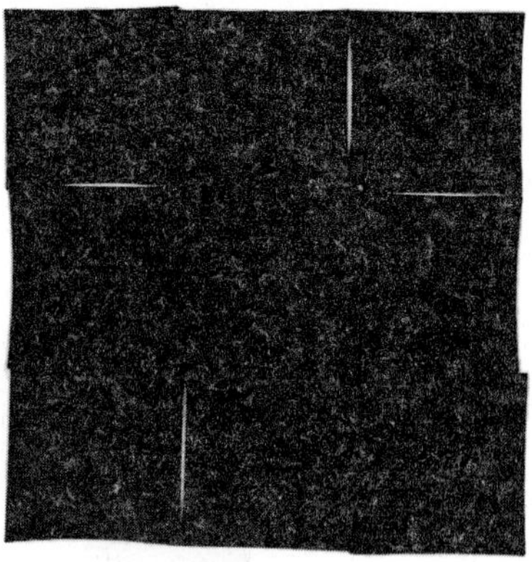

2a)

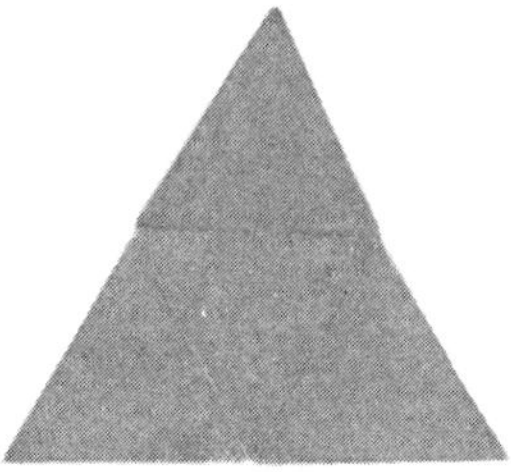

2b)

3a)

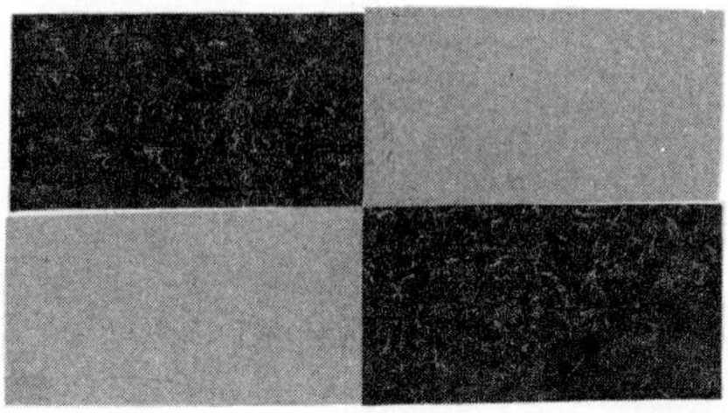

3b)

Alan Sutcliffe

Teachers with special interests in say music, road safety, or different types of sports and games can similarly work out networks relating mathematics to their areas of interest and expertise.

And Reality

> ... for many pupils, probably most, the beauty of abstract pattern and the precision of logic have less appeal than the possibility of applying mathematics to 'real life situations.'[10]

Some mathematics educators believe that almost all children can think like mathematicians and can take naturally to the processes of classifying, hypothesizing verifying, generalizing, explaining and proving.

Probably most pure mathematicians would argue that utility as a goal is inferior to the pursuit of beauty and elegance. However, for the majority of school pupils, it is the application of mathematics to real life situations which are of more interest.

With regard to other subject areas in the curriculum the two subjects which probably most naturally provide links with mathematics are environmental studies and science. The links between environmental studies and mathematics for the first school have been well developed by Margaret Collis.[11] Using some of her ideas, a scheme which analyzes the mathematics which might naturally arise from a visit to a farm is included.

In the secondary school, science and mathematics syllabuses are sometimes developed by the members of the different departments working in isolation. It may even be the case in some primary schools where the same teacher teaches both subject areas, that science and mathematics syllabuses are drawn up without considering the natural links which exist between the two subject areas.

When teaching science in primary schools we are interested in the utilitarian value of mathematics to support our experiments. We proceed inductively from the specific situations to the generalizations. We realize that mathematics provides us with a powerful means of communication about our explorations with real situations and concrete materials. These experimental situations are normally measuring, rather than counting situations. They use decimals (rational numbers) rather than counting numbers (natural numbers). As with all measurement work, the skills of estimation and approximation are of paramount importance.

Alan Sutcliffe

FARM VISIT

PLACE OR ACTIVITY	VOCABULARY	CONTENT
1 *In the farmyard*		
(a) gate at entrance	rectangle, triangle, parallel lines, horizontal, vertical, rotation, axis	recognition of 2D shapes, sets of lines, congruence, transformation
(b) sheep in pen	one, two, three ...	counting, cardinal number, conservation of number
(c) stack of pipes (tiles)	cylinders, hollow, rows, circles	recognition of 3D shapes, triangular numbers $1 + 2 + 3 + 4 \ldots$
2 *In the barn*		
(a) bales of hay	cuboid	recognition of 3D shapes
(b) elevator	lift, higher than	translation (shape, size, orientation preserved)
(c) roof trusses	triangles	recognition of 2D shapes
(d) windows	square corners	angles
3 *In the byre or milking parlour*		
(a) cows in stalls	two in a stall, pairs	many-to-one, correspondence, grouping
(b) large and small containers	holds more than, less than, litres	capacity standard units
4 *In the fields*		
(a) different animals	sheep, horses, animals, taller than, longer than	sets of animals, inclusion relation, relations
(b) fences, fields	inside, outside, primeter, enclosure, larger than, smaller area than	neighbourhood
5 *Collecting things*		
(a) coats	feathers, wool, hair, belongs to	sets of coats relations
(b) eggs	filling the basket medium, large, sixes collect, sort, box	tessellation, mass grouping, multiplication sequencing

Mathematics Across the Curriculum

Again we need to be aware of both the children's stages of mathematical development and the hierarchy of skills and concepts in mathematics. Important skills in science are the communicating and recording and the interpretation of the results of experimental work. Pictorial and graphical work will arise naturally from such experiences. The use of data from experiences in science will help children to make the difficult transition from pictorial representation, where there is no obvious relationship, to graphs where there is a definite relationship.

As an example of how different contexts in science can relate to the same concepts in mathematics the following situations have been taken from a primary school science syllabus and relate to the mathematical concept of proportion (or equality between ratios). This graphical approach to the concept of proportion through activities in science contrasts with the practical approach to the related concept of scale referred to earlier. At this stage we are leading up to, in a more abstract manner, a mathematical model of the different scientific situations.

Plant Studies

The behaviour of seeds and bulbs germinating and growing is often observed. Measurements are made using appropriate units and to an appropriate degree of accuracy. Sunflowers and amyrillis can be relied upon to grow in a regular fashion over a reasonable time scale.

After some discussion regarding independent and dependent variables and choice of suitable scales, heights can be plotted against time. Questions can be asked regarding the steadiness of the growth and the rate of growth.

Predictions about the growth at a certain point in time can be made and checked and amended if necessary.

Structures and Forces

Bridge building activities can lead to a comparison of thickness of material and the load which can be carried for the same bridge design. If we maintain the difference between the supports, the more paper rods of standard thickness we use, the stronger the bridge will be. Similarly when stretching springs children should be able to discover that, within limits, the stretch depends directly upon the load carried by the spring.

Alan Sutcliffe

Tools and Machines

When studying the gears and cogs of bicycles it can be discovered that the distance travelled forward by a bicycle for a given number of turns of the pedal cranks depends upon the gear of the bicycle (is directly proportional to the size of the gear).[12]

These experimental situations illustrate the mathematical concept of proportion. In general terms, if we double, treble (or multiply by a constant K) the independent variable then the dependent variable will double, treble (or multiply by a constant K). The graphs of the related variables will be approximations to a straight line through the origin. The relationship may be expressed, within limits, by the mathematical model $y = kx$ or $y_1/x_1 = y_2/x_2$ Research has shown that this concept is a difficult one for many secondary school children.[13] By providing concrete examples in different contexts in primary schools difficulties which children experience at the secondary stage may be reduced.

Conclusion

The term 'mathematics across the curriculum' may originally have been coined by the Open University when developing a course of the same name.[14] Perhaps a better title for this course would have been 'Real Problem Solving'. The pilot study for the course, carried out in Walsall, has been well documented.[15]

The problems used, such as 'Shall we retain the tuck shop' and 'Can playtime be made more enjoyable' were 'real' in that they were provided by primary school children. Their solutions had some pay off in terms of action to improve conditions. Whole classes were involved and the problems were refined by the children into areas for investigation. An account of a project which developed from the Open University notion of real problem solving is also available.[16]

This chapter has placed a different interpretation upon the term 'mathematics across the curriculum'. It has aimed to heighten the reader's awareness of where mathematics occurs naturally in other parts of the primary school curriculum.

At the nursery and infant level mathematics occurs naturally in many play and topic contexts. A teacher with the necessary mathematical background can use these situations, many of which occur incidentally, to develop the children's mathematical experience and understanding. It has also been suggested that other curriculum areas, and teachers' special interests, frequently provide contexts for the development of children's mathematical skills and concepts. Science and orienteering were chosen as examples. Comments, suggestions and details of readers' experiences in teaching 'mathematics across the curriculum' would be gratefully received.

Notes and References

1 DEPARTMENT OF EDUCATION AND SCIENCE (1985) *Mathematics from 5 to 16*, London, HMSO.
2 SCHOOLS COUNCIL (1978) *Early Mathematical Experiences*, London, Addison Wesley.
3 MATTHEWS, J (1973) *Progress Records for Young Children*, London, Chambers/Murray.
4 DEPARTMENT OF EDUCATION AND SCIENCE (1985) *op cit.*
5 COCKCROFT, WH (1982) *Report of the Committee of Enquiry into the Teaching of Mathematics in Schools: Mathematics Counts*, London, HMSO.
6 ASSOCIATION OF TEACHERS OF MATHEMATICS (1983) *Teaching Styles — A Response to Cockcroft*, Derby, Association of Teachers of Mathematics.
7 British Orienteering Federation, Riversdale, Dale Road North, Darley Dale, Matlock, Derbyshire, DE4 2JB. Packs for schools: Come Orienteering.
8 Silva Compass (London) Ltd, 76 Broad Street, Teddington, Middlesex, TW11 8QT.
9 MCNEILL, C and RENFREW, T (1985) *Introducing and Developing Orienteering in the Primary School*, Strathclyde, Strathclyde Department of Education.
10 BAUSOR, J (1974) 'Mathematics and science: Uneasy truce or open hostilities?', *Mathematics Teaching*, 68.
11 COLLIS, M (1974) *Using the Environment: 1 Early Explorations*, Schools Council 5/13 Project, London, Macdonald Educational.
12 NEWTON, WF (1978) 'Bicycle mathematics', *Maths in Schools*, 7, 5.
13 HART, KM (Ed) (1981) *Children's Understanding of Mathematics*, London, John Murray.
14 OPEN UNIVERSITY (1980), *Mathematics Across the Curriculum*, PME 233, Milton Keynes, Open University Press.
15 'Mathematics across the curriculum', *Times Educational Supplement Extra*, 9 May 1980.
16 HAYLOCK, DW, BLAKE, GF and PLATT, J (1985) 'Using maths to make things happen', *Maths in School*, 14, 2.

'Is It An Add, Miss?': Mathematics in the Early Primary Years

Toni McPherson and Gill Payne

Introduction

In this chapter many of the key issues which affect the development of mathematical education in the primary school are discussed in relation to the early primary years. Some of the important questions that are raised are considered in detail and the implications of those questions for teachers of young children are explored. In considering the 'new directions' that mathematics teaching has taken in recent years and the curriculum development that is currently being considered, the aim is always towards reaching an 'ideal' position but this often places enormous pressure on the class teacher who has to take account of the many conflicting demands on her time and her energy. In this chapter no easy answers are offered. We only succeed in raising some of the questions that teachers of young children are expected to address.

Central Control and a Core Curriculum

There seems to be a strong move towards central control of the curriculum. An example of one of these moves is the framework set out for discussion in *Mathematics 5–16*[1] which could impose considerable restrictions on the way that teachers work. This might well lead to a conflict between having to teach set content, at least to the extent of having a common core of content, and the freedom to choose what to teach and how to teach it.

> Perhaps the idea that school can give all pupils the same education ... is not well founded. A more feasible alterna-

tive would be to give every pupil the education he needs and can assimilate.[2]

In these days of equal opportunity it may well be heresy to suggest that it is not necessarily appropriate for all children to be given exactly the same experience but rather that the experience should be able to match the previous learning and the abilities of each child. It could be that a differential curriculum would be more appropriate with a common core of content that is offered to all children and an opportunity for extension of that core for the more able or interested pupil. Desforges[3] suggests that middle or high attainers are able to cope effectively with a broader curriculum but that the lower attainers could not cope with the breadth.

Mathematics is said to be a hierarchical subject in as much as a child might find learning new mathematical skills difficult, if not impossible, if he has not learnt the relevant preceding facts and skills. If this is so then there is less conflict created by the imposition of national guidelines because it seems likely that progression through the mathematical study areas would be less negotiable.

Learning mathematics could be more successful if all children were given the opportunity to gain competence in a limited number of mathematical areas whilst the more able were then encouraged to extend the range of topics considered and the depth at which they were covered. It could well be that in working successfully on a more limited range of topics the less able are given greater confidence. This could have the added benefit of producing more positive attitudes to mathematics.

Obviously in the long run it is the school and the teachers within the school who make the decisions about what is to be taught and the strategies that will be most appropriate but there are several factors that will affect their choices. One of these factors is the present interest of the DES and the various initiatives that they have taken to influence curriculum developments.

The objectives listed in *Mathematics 5–16*[4] suggest that certain areas of content are appropriate to the 'average' child. However, the document also accepts the existence of 'the seven-year difference' of the *Cockcroft Report*[5] and therefore implies that teachers have freedom within their classrooms to plan the curriculum, teach the content and assess the children in their own way. It is the teacher who knows the children in her class. Education is only successful if the individuals are learning. Teachers have, therefore, to find ways of encouraging children to develop mathematically at their own rates although they may be organized to carry out tasks individually, in pairs, in small groups or in large groups. *Education Observed*[6] stated that:

> Modest academic performance may represent, for some pupils, a significant learning gain in relation to earlier achievements or to a background of disadvantage or deprivation. Each individual pupil's achievement at the end of a phase of schooling has to be judged in the light of his ability and his performance on entering that phase.

Parental and Community Expectations

The role of teachers has changed in many ways over recent years to the extent that they are being pulled in many directions at once. Teachers now have to include more liaison with parents, more 'open door' policy teaching, more pastoral care and more responsibility for the moral welfare of the children (ranging from teaching table manners to teaching about the dangers of drug and solvent abuse!).

With accountability at every level in today's educational structure, planning and implementing the curriculum has become a publicly scrutinized process. Teachers must be sure of their objectives and be able to convince those who are scrutinizing of the value of those objectives.

There seems to be agreement about the minimum amount of mathematical knowledge which an adult needs to 'get by'. Beyond this, however, different bodies in the community have different expectations. Many adults think of mathematics in terms of numeracy and consider computational skills as the most important. Some employers would like to see specific skills being taught in schools but, on the whole, employers seem reasonably satisfied with school mathematics today. *Mathematics Counts*[7] says that 'Only 14 per cent (of 300 employers surveyed) criticized the educational standards of their recruits. More ... criticisms found ... were of inability to take work seriously, lack of interest, unwillingness to work, bad time keeping and poor attendance.'

Parents are naturally very concerned that their children strive towards their maximum potential. Today's educational system still assesses that potential by the number of 'O' levels, GCSE and 'A' level examination passes held by the child. They are the wise parents who recognize the limitations of their children and look for

Mathematics in the Early Primary Years

attainable examination targets and success in other life skills which will stand their children in greater stead on leaving school. In the early years the implication of this is that teachers and parents should be able to negotiate which skills are important, life skills not just mathematical ones. 'Back to basics' need not be the cry from a reasonable parent body which has been informed sensibly about curriculum planning and the objectives of the school.

Primary Practice[8] comments that ' ... parental interest is stimulated by open evenings and invitations to assemblies, carol services, concerts and exhibitions. All these activities help to promote understanding and support.'

The Importance of the Early Years

The years of a child's development before he ever goes to school, are widely recognized as being the time when the foundations for later learning are laid. *Mathematics 5–16* states that 'The early stages of learning mathematics are of crucial importance.' It is generally recognized that before they begin statutory schooling, most children will already have encountered many everyday situations which require them to use mathematical language and to demonstrate mathematical thinking.

There is considerable evidence that young children can display 'impressive mathematical abilities'[9] and can be competent in dealing with quite complex problems in a logical way. Most pre-school age children begin to develop their mathematical understanding in a wide variety of natural settings, at home and in other social contexts. That understanding comes from the need to solve many problems in everyday life, handling numerical data, understanding relationships and appreciating pattern, shape and symmetry. For these children 'mathematics' is a practical activity totally integrated into and necessitated by their life experience. For example they are likely to go shopping and to see parents and shop assistants handling money. They come to appreciate that there are a variety of coins which have value and that expensive items may well be out of reach! They may go to the Post Office or to the bank to collect money.

Number symbols are also on view in many aspects of the child's everyday life, the number 9 bus may take him to the shops, he may be '4 years old today' or he may live at house number 65. If he has been to nursery school or playgroup he should also have had additional, carefully planned experience which would increase his opportunity to make sense of his mathematical experiences. He may well have played the number rhymes and games that used to be an integral part of every child's play. These seem to be less popular today, but television advertising jingles and signature tunes are the modern equivalents and they also refer to numbers and mathematical relationships.

Mathematics and Starting School

> School mathematics ... should be based on and linked to the understanding of number which children possess when they start school.[10]

On entry to school these same children may well find that the mathematics that they are being 'taught' bears little or no relation to the ideas that they had already understood in the pre-school context. The mathematical processes may be the same but they are frequently presented through abstract methods and materials. Some of the difficulties which young children seem to have with learning mathematics in school may arise from the fact that this range of early experience is not being capitalized upon or incorporated into the first school curriculum. Often the existing and well developed capabilities of young school children remain untapped or unrecognized. Even where their understanding is not ignored it is often considerably underestimated. This aspect of mismatch and the consequent lack of continuity for the child could make it more difficult for him to learn mathematics. If he is finding difficulty then this could affect his attitude and hence his performance.

The report by HMI *Education 5–9*[11] found that high priority was given to mathematics teaching in first schools but that this was frequently at the level of computation and the rote learning of algorithms, without regard to the practical applications of those ideas. 'Younger children were as likely to practise mathematical skills in isolation as were the older children.'

Consequently, children may well be competent in applying an algorithm in a specific situation and they may be accurate in completing that specific task yet have no understanding of why that particular formula is used or of the general concepts that are involved. They are then unable to transfer their learning from a specific situation to its use in solving a 'real', practical problem.

Mathematics as a Problem Solving Activity

> The ability to solve problems is at the heart of mathematics.[12]

In preparing children for the world of the future it seems likely that they will need to be mentally agile to adapt the processes that they have understood and the skills that they have acquired to a variety of changing situations. It also seems likely that they will need to recognize parallels between different processes and see significant similarities and differences where they occur. Acquiring strategies to 'get started' on finding the solution to a problem can be a major hurdle for many children. It may be that drawing a picture, looking for a pattern, acting it out, having a guess and then finding how far out that is out, looking for more clues in the question and then asking and posing further questions to start a logical train of thought are all possible paths through the problem solving process. Questions then arise as to which path is the most sensible and an evaluation of the relative merits of all the solutions is necessary.

As children become more aware of appropriate methods and strategies, their problem solving abilities will increase. This is not to advocate a return to the 'laissez faire' discovery situations where children were left to 'find out' for themselves but rather a cooperative effort with the teacher guiding and nudging a child or group of children through to a set of conclusions which are mathematically satisfactory.

Confidence

> The overall climate of a school can contribute greatly to learning motivation and to good discipline. Teachers need to work together to create an atmosphere of confidence and consideration.[13]

Most teachers are trying to create a happy, relaxed, and non-threatening atmosphere within their classrooms but at the same time they wish to present activities which are both motivating and challenging. If a child finds a solution to a problem, which at the outset appeared to be difficult, if not impossible, then he or she experiences moments of triumph and elation. Those are the moments which influence the child's attitudes and those moments need to be noted both by the child, and by others so that he becomes consciously aware of his new found knowledge and 'knows what he knows'. Giving a child the opportunity to have an audience for his or her work puts a value on the effort and on the achievement and thus builds up the child's self-confidence and self-esteem.

These moments of success and achievement should not be judged by just the 'answer' or conclusion reached but by the processes passed through, by the perseverance and persistence shown by the child and by the creativity and resourcefulness displayed.

> At every level in the teaching of mathematics the formation of concepts should have priority over the acquisition of technical skills. This is not to imply that such skills are to be neglected, but that emphasis on understanding will facilitate the acquisition of those skills which are needed.[14]

Both *Mathematics Counts* and *Mathematics 5–16* highlight the need for children to work cooperatively, to have the opportunities for mathematical discussion amongst themselves, and to work independently:

> Working cooperatively is not a skill only for the maths lesson. Asking questions of peers and listening to and considering their answers is a social skill much needed in this world.[15]

This supports the practice used in many early years classrooms where, on different occasions, the children may be working on individual assignments, in pairs, which Bruner suggested might be the best size of working group, or in small groups of four to six children on an assignment which necessitates their discussing the processes involved and cooperatively negotiating the methods which they will adopt. They may sometimes be working as a class, planning a cooperative venture or providing an audience for the children to display their achievements. If it is accepted that the process of solving problems or answering questions is at least as important as the final outcome, then the record of the activity must, equally, take many forms. It may well be a page of written work but it may, quite frequently not be in written form at all. The child may produce a small display of his own creation, a tape recording of his findings, an oral 'story' to illustrate his understanding of the procedures involved, a printout of his work on a computer, a set of questions for another member of the class on a particular topic or even simply an 'aura' of confidence created by the successful completion of a practical task which has no permanent record except the sight of a child running happily home to recall his mathematical successes.

Workbooks and workcards can have a place when consolidation and practice of particular skills are needed but written pages cannot teach new understanding. It is the teacher's role to set up situations in which a child will encounter new experiences and acquire new understanding. These experiences should initially be of a practical nature, along with discussion and plenty of time to allow the child to ask questions. This helps him to reorganize his own mental imagery of his mathematical world. It is only when the teacher finds the time to assess the child's thinking that she can then identify areas where the child has misunderstood or is forming an inaccurate schema for his mathematical thinking. If initial learning is to take place in practical and oral situations then the implication is that written recording will not begin when the child first enters school, indeed it may not occur until well into the second, third or even fourth term at school. When 'formal' written work does begin then it will be as a record of clearly understood ideas.

The Place of Rote Learning

There is much discussion about the value of rote learning. Its value is suspect when children are committing facts to memory which are not understood. However it cannot be denied, that by having access to a bank of number facts which can be instantly recalled, a child is not held back or demoralized by the sheer difficulties of the computations involved. He can rise to a greater level of understanding and will gain greater rewards as he is able to tackle more complicated problems. However, although a bank of mathematical facts stored permanently in one's memory is undeniably useful and desirable, a bank of algorithms may often be unhelpful. Many successful adults will remember their schooldays when getting the right answer meant doing the set procedure. They did not know why a method worked but they accepted it, used it and sometimes understanding dawned many years later. Without the understanding of the processes involved in a problem many children will not know which algorithm to use. A hesitant hand will be raised and he will mutter 'Is it an add, Miss?'. He might reason 'More than means add so when I want to answer "Mary has £3 now, how much more does she need to buy a radio for £11?" I had better add!'.

Young children today will be coping with an unknown future.

Algorithms we might teach today may well be inappropriate for the future. Mental agility is far more important as a preparation for that future. A child must have the ability to call upon facts which he knows, processes he has mastered and skills which he has acquired. When faced with new problems he must be able to see parallels where they occur and find the differences from previous problems and experiences in order that he can apply his understanding in a new way.

Assessment of Pupils

Assessing a child's current stage of development accurately is essential for planning his next and future tasks. Teachers need to be able to formulate expectations for each child so that they can provide the best match between tasks set and the child's stage of development and also predict which activities will prove challenging and rewarding for that child. *Primary Practice*[15] states, 'Finding a match between the difficulty of learning material and each child's development is among a teacher's most necessary skills.'

Teacher expectations should be as accurate as possible; not only for the planning of the programme of work for a child but also to build up the self-esteem and confidence of the child. Nash[16] refers to 'a community of knowledge' held by pupils and teachers about the relative ability of every member of the class. If everyone around him expect him to fail then the self-esteem of the child decreases and his achievement level may also decrease.

Teachers are continually amassing hundreds of facts about the children in their care. All these facts play a part in the planning of the programme of work for that child but only some of that information will find its way into the child's school record.

Staff can work together within their school and liaise with other schools to create a simple but effective system of record keeping. Agreement can be reached on content, format and criteria for assessment to ensure both continuity within a school and easier transition between schools. Records which will not be read prove to be a source of irritation and an insult to the teacher who wrote them. Too little information may not give a true picture of the child and too much data would prove too time consuming for the teacher assessing the child and would probably not be read by subsequent teachers. A recording system should be planned which has a balance between these factors.

Mathematics in the Early Primary Years

There is difficulty in assessing and recording progress in discussion skills, problem solving abilities, powers of observation and the willingness to work cooperatively. These assessments are as important for ensuring continuity of the learning process as the systems of assessment currently in use. Ways can be found to record these important abilities to the satisfaction of those needing to use the record.

It is also desirable that the teacher is aware of the general standards of attainment not only outside her classroom but also outside her school and for her to be aware of the achievements of children of similar ages and backgrounds. The work of the assessment of performance unit can help here as well as the occasional use of some standardized tests. *Mathematics 5–16*[7] states 'Standardized tests have their uses but need to be complemented by other methods of assessment'. Such tests can only hint at the difficulties being experienced by a particular child, but they are not probing enough to be diagnostic in themselves. When used on record cards, and passed on to the next teacher, there is always a danger that a standardized score for a child may pre-set the teacher's expectations of that child. Again a balance has to be found between 'subjective' assessments made currently by teachers, agreed 'assessment tests' and standardized scores. They all add to the general 'picture' of the child and his learning ability.

The Teacher

One of the joys of teaching in the early years is that the teacher has the control over how the agreed content is taught. Currently, desired mathematical objectives include:

(a) trying to make mathematics a practical subject;
(b) making mathematics more relevant to the real world;
(c) encouraging children to work cooperatively;
(d) providing opportunities for children to talk mathematically;
(e) organizing times when children are able to reflect on their efforts or will have an audience for their work and hence develop their confidence and self-esteem.

When attempting to create an atmosphere in which children successfully learn mathematics with enjoyment, a teacher may have to face a whole series of conflicting pressures. These may relate to the teaching style adopted, to the expectations from the parent body and from the community in general, to the organizational problems associated with the agreed aims and objectives or to the confidence and expertise of the teacher.

It is generally accepted that no two classes are the same; differences such as the children's abilities and interests, their social interaction and personalities and even the weather, will combine to create the learning atmosphere of that class at that moment in time. Teachers are continually adapting, changing, adding to and even abandoning the prepared lesson plans as they assess the suitability of the work. They assess by monitoring the reactions of the children, looking at the eagerness of their responses, and at the 'light in their eyes':

> Within the carefully planned syllabus, or individual lesson, the confident and competent teacher will recognise the need for a spontaneous response either to an external event or to a surge of interest and excitement from the pupils themselves. The ability to capitalise on the unexpected and to turn it into learning which is creative and enjoyable is one of the marks of the good and enjoyable teacher.[18]

With so many innovations, suggested changes of approach and style, new schemes being published and national criteria being introduced in all subject areas, it is no wonder that many teachers of early years classes are feeling varying degrees of panic. Few are mathematicians and many are insecure about their mathematical knowledge. Many rely on published schemes, which have already been thought out by 'experts', to provide ideas and continuity for their teaching programme.

Some teachers, while reasonably confident about teaching computation and measuring skills feel very threatened and insecure at the thought of leaving the published scheme, to introduce investigations and problem solving. 'What,' they ask, 'if the children wander off into an avenue of mathematics I do not understand?', 'What if they ask questions that I cannot answer?', 'What if I give them answers which turn out to be incorrect because I don't have enough knowledge myself?'. These questions and doubts are natural and show a healthy ability to evaluate oneself. It is unrealistic to expect all teachers to be 'experts' in all subject areas. But if these same teachers believe that certain changes in their teaching style might bring an improvement in the children's ability to learn and use mathematics they must find ways to overcome their uncertainties. It is only when teachers are generally confident in a subject that they are prepared to admit to children that they don't know all the answers.

Teacher assessment will automatically include an element of self-evaluation together with assessment from at least one other person. Once weaknesses are identified, either by oneself or by others, there should be an immediate demand for some form of improvement programme.

The Role of the Mathematics Coordinator

The mathematics consultant or coordinator in a school or group of schools is given the task of organizing and planning for the development, and the implementation and subsequent evaluation of the mathematics curriculum in the school. 'Such teachers may give support in a variety of ways: by producing guidelines and schemes of work; by leading discussions and organizing study groups; by disseminating work done on in-service courses; by working alongside class teachers; by assembling and organizing resources; and occasionally by teaching classes other than their own.'[19] Their special task is to provide specific understanding and support in a cooperative and non-threatening way so as to improve the quality of the mathematics teaching in the school.

The effective coordinator will ensure that there is liaison between each class in the school, promoting comparability between classes and continuity between stages within a school and between schools. Through discussion with the teachers an appropriate curriculum will be planned to take account of the needs of individual children and of the groups within a class. Obviously it would be very beneficial if every school had a coordinator for mathematics whose advice could be sought when appropriate. In practice this is not always possible.

Cooperation Between Schools

Over recent years school rolls have fallen and staff numbers have decreased. 'Natural wastage' may well have meant the loss of the mathematics coordinator who cannot be replaced. Alternatively there are many schools in rural areas with only two or three members of staff. Circumstances could well dictate that there is not a mathematics specialist among them. The lack of a coordinator, through no fault in planning or appointing, might also undermine the confidence of the staff when evaluating mathematical innovations. Cooperation between schools could help overcome this problem. The most effective cooperation group may prove to be schools which are in close proximity, where not only staff but children can get together to widen their experiences. Within such a group of staff there may be a 'specialist', by training, experience or inclination, who will be able to give support to the others.

In-Service

In-service courses provide another way to learn about new ideas and to give time to reflect upon and evaluate possible innovations. The new system for the funding of in-service courses creates the exciting opportunity for schools to bid for supply cover for one, or more (possibly all) of the staff to plan their in-service needs. They might attend courses in recognized centres or create their own programme within school. Schools can request help for input from advisers, advisory teachers or colleges of higher education. Advisory teachers can be requested to work alongside teachers in their own classrooms, demonstrating and disseminating new ideas.

Teachers may also benefit from having student teachers in their schools on teaching practice. The practice may enable teachers to see some new ideas and can create an atmosphere in which teachers talk through and evaluate their current aims in mathematical education. There is a new wave of partnership evolving between teacher education tutors and teachers. Whichever method for staff development is found it is valuable for teachers to familiarize themselves with recent trends and research findings as well as becoming aware of the availability of new resources or the new uses of old apparatus. No teacher can take everything on board, nor make too many changes too quickly. However, without knowledge of the ideas, evaluations cannot decide which, if any, of the ideas may be worth investigating further or introducing into the classroom.

Organization

Mathematics 5–16[20] states that 'The organization of pupils, the deployment of staff, the writing of schemes of work and the use of resources and accommodation are important issues for all schools'.

Creating a classroom climate in which mathematical growth and creativity can take place may pose several organizational problems for the class teacher, problems of not having enough time, enough pairs of hands, enough space and equipment.

One of the first priorities might well be to find ways to free the teacher to discuss work with an individual child or with a group of children. This freedom can occur if the children have developed the ability to work independently. There is a need to encourage children to take responsibility for their own work, to be able to organize themselves and to develop the ability to decide 'what to do next' when the initial task is completed.

Problem solving activities can prove a valuable aid in freeing the teacher. If children are presented with real problems in contextual situations with which they can identify they will more readily understand and be able to work independently of the teacher for some time. They will still need the checks and discussions which teachers provide as they walk around the classroom monitoring the work in progress. The teacher is there to ask the right questions at the right moments during the problem solving process. It is the skilled teacher who knows when to intervene and when to stay quiet but without that intervention many children might not find a solution or might not be able to evaluate, modify or improve their ideas.

Freeing the teacher may have implications for the organization of the resources and equipment within the classroom. Much teacher time is absorbed monitoring equipment. There are classes where the close monitoring of equipment is essential but to have trained professionals performing such tasks is not a cost-effective use of manpower.

Reorganization of resources might also include a rearrangement of the classroom furniture. Many infant classrooms have children grouped at tables and this organization hopefully encourages cooperative learning and promotes discussion. Classes frequently come together 'on the carpet' to discuss and show each other the achievements of the day but are there also opportunities for children to sit in pairs or on their own if the desire or need arises.

There is nothing more disheartening than for a child to be engrossed in a problem or activity and be told to stop because 'It's time to go out to play' or 'It's time to go to television'. Obviously it is not acceptable for a child to be left unattended or to miss the television input on which other lessons may well be based. Can ways be found around this problem? Can the school day be flexible? Can teachers work cooperatively and supervise each other's children?

Can the child simply be allowed to continue after the interruption and not have to pack away his work until the next 'maths' lesson by which time he will have lost his train of thought and probably his motivation as well?

Reorganization may result in the instigation of major changes. Some staff may wish to work in a team-teaching situation. Others may not, but may, nevertheless, wish to cooperate with another teacher for some parts of the week and thus reap some of the benefits that cooperative teaching can achieve. Other teachers may wish to find another pair of hands to assist in the classroom; headteachers, for example, who are not committed to a class may offer their expertise, current ancillary help can relieve the teacher of many of the time consuming tasks that she has to do, including helping with monitoring equipment, checking on children going to the toilet, assisting with spellings and so on. Although this help is not usually full time and will therefore not overcome many of the problems of flexibility it will of course help.

Parents as Partners

Particularly in the early years learning is very much a partnership between home and school. Parents, as partners, are becoming very evident in today's classrooms they are often seen as invaluable helpers. They may supervise children in art and craft activities, they may read stories and discuss the plots with a group of children, they may oversee children having a 'free play' session in the water trough; they may carry out some routine task to help the busy teacher and, on occasions, they may hear readers but, so often, they shy away from wanting to help with any mathematics or mathematical situation.

Parents are frequently aware that mathematics teaching is very different today. They often lack confidence in either their own knowledge of mathematics or in today's methods of teaching the subject. They may even need to be introduced to the pleasures that the subject can give. Children learn a great deal by copying either their peers or the adults in their lives. How often do they see a parent, or even a teacher, actually doing mathematics? More and more parents are realizing that to help their child all that is often needed is more of what they are already doing at home.

Parents are in a position in which a teacher can rarely be — that of a one-to-one relationship with a child for many hours a day.

Some parents may wish to have it explained to them that many everyday experiences and discussions provide the solid foundations on which a teacher can build the children's mathematical futures; experiences such as playing with water, cooking, playing board games, laying the table and having discussions, for example, about what is happening in the world, the shapes around them, the time it takes to get somewhere, tomorrow's visit by the doctor or granny's visit next Tuesday. The realization of the important and essential role that parents can play in the mathematical development of their children will often make available sources of expertise previously untapped and create a partnership from which the children, the teacher and the parents all reap great benefits.

Conclusion

The new directions in the teaching of mathematics in the early years give teachers a great deal to reflect upon. However, there are many externally imposed conditions which affect the freedom of teachers to select and implement changes. They are subject to LEA contracts, pressures from advisers, the leadership within the school, the organization of the school and the nature of the pupils and of the community served.

A View of The Curriculum states that:

> There are limits of resources, both generally and in individual schools. ... There are limits to what can be done. There are limits of time, in the day, in the week, in the year, in the span of compulsory education as a whole. Children cannot be forearmed with everything they need to know or be able to do as adults, even if they were already to receive it. There must always be some selection.[21]

All concerned with education should accept that it is unrealistic to expect teachers, to achieve everything. The aim shall be to strive for the ideal but there are limits to the possible.

Notes and References

1 DEPARTMENT OF EDUCATION AND SCIENCE (1985) *Mathematics from 5 to 16,* London, HMSO.
2 HUGHES, M (1986) *Children and Number,* London, Ward Lock.

3 DESFORGES, C (1983) *Quality of Pupil Learning Experience*, London, Longmans.
4 DEPARTMENT OF EDUCATION AND SCIENCE (1985) *op cit.*
5 COCKCROFT, WH (1982) *Report of the Committee of Enquiry into the Teaching of Mathematics in Schools: Mathematics Counts*, London, HMSO.
6 DEPARTMENT OF EDUCATION AND SCIENCE *Education Observed*, London, HMSO.
7 COCKCROFT, WH (1982) *op cit.*
8 SCHOOLS COUNCIL (1983) *Primary Practice*, London, Methuen.
9 HUGHES, M (1986) *op cit.*
10 *Ibid.*
11 DEPARTMENT OF EDUCATION AND SCIENCE (1983) *Education 5–9*, London, HMSO.
12 COCKCROFT, WH (1982) *op cit.*
13 DEPARTMENT OF EDUCATION AND SCIENCE (1985) *op cit.*
14 DEPARTMENT OF EDUCATION AND SCIENCE (1980) *A View of the Curriculum*, London, HMSO.
15 SCHOOLS COUNCIL (1983) *op cit.*
16 NASH, R (1973) *Classrooms Observed*, London Routledge and Kegan Paul.
17 DEPARTMENT OF EDUCATION AND SCIENCE (1985) *op cit.*
18 DEPARTMENT OF EDUCATION AND SCIENCE (1985) *Education Observed*, London, HMSO.
19 DEPARTMENT OF EDUCATION AND SCIENCE (1983) *op cit.*
20 DEPARTMENT OF EDUCATION AND SCIENCE (1985) *op cit.*
21 DEPARTMENT OF EDUCATION AND SCIENCE (1980) *op cit.*

Mathematics in the Junior Years

Chris Bailey

Publications and Advice

During the past ten years teachers have been inundated with advice, recommendations and directives on what they should be teaching and how it should be done (*Mathematics from 5 to 11*; *Mathematics Counts*; *Mathematics from 5 to 16*; APU reports). The result is confusion rather than clarity; confusion due to conflicting advice and to the quantity of literature that must be assimilated.

When a report or discussion document becomes too general it is relatively easy for the reader to relate the recommendations to their existing practice and thus for the 'status quo' to be preserved. The Cockcroft Report unwittingly contributed to this when advocating different styles of teaching including exposition, discussion, practical activities, practice, problem solving and investigational work. The emphasis in the Cockcroft Report is on the variety of styles which should be adopted according to the topic and the abilities and experiences of teachers and pupils. However, many teachers seeing their method in the list of styles continue to rely solely on their tried and tested approach to teaching maths, in the mistaken belief that they are right and that their method is supported by current literature. In any event few teachers have the time or energy to read the plethora of reports in detail. In the same way that many a student has managed to pass his examination by reading only the aims and conclusions of the work of some or other authority, teachers in general only read the abridged versions of reports to be found in the *Times Educational Supplement* or other professional journals. The DES accepted this in the case of the Cockcroft Report by publishing its own abridged pamphlet.

The numerous reports and discussion documents are all part of the accountability process and are designed to make teachers more aware of the needs of education's consumers. According to Cockcroft[1] the mathematical needs of adult life include 'the ability to read numbers and to count, to tell the time, to pay for purchases and to give change, to weigh and measure, to understand straightforward timetables and simple graphs and charts and to carry out any necessary calculations associated with these'. The emphasis on the practical nature of these activities provides the cornerstone of relevant, practical experiences (*Mathematics 5–11*)[2] on which children's mathematical development should be built. There is, urge these reports, still too great an emphasis on pencil and paper activities in the teaching of mathematics in junior schools. Practical activities and the use of apparatus are too frequently scorned in favour of problem solving which has no relevance to everyday life and is merely computation with words. The need to think of the consumers when we teach mathematics and ensure that what is taught is relevant to their futures is a cornerstone of much that is being urged in the teaching of mathematics.

Advisory Teachers

Teachers need practical support and guidance related to their individual schools and circumstances if there is to be a real improvement in the standard and quality of mathematics teaching. Given that many primary teachers still do not have a specific qualification in mathematics, and consequently lack confidence in their own ability, it is imperative that personal support is available. The introduction of advisory teachers with the emphasis on their advisory capacity is an important step forward. The LEA advisers for primary mathematics tend to be thought of as inspectors and are often designated as such rather than advisers and therefore are not readily approached by teachers in difficulties with teaching mathematics. In contrast, the advisory teacher is seen as an ally who will encourage experimentation and foster confidence.

In 1984 only 14 per cent of LEAs had advisory teachers. Recently the majority of education authorities have appointed one or two advisory teachers with specific responsibilities for primary maths. This is a direct consequence of the initiative taken by the DES to offer education support grants for the teaching of maths. The role of the advisory teacher is specifically designed to encourage good classroom practice. The advisory teacher is expected to work

Mathematics in the Junior Years

in the classroom with teachers, to encourage staff development and to advise schools on its mathematics education policy and the use of resources.

Advisory teachers are in an ideal position for forging links with neighbouring authorities so that ideas, experiments and examples of good practice can be shared and disseminated more widely rather than developed and duplicated within each local authority. Many advisory teachers are creating mathematics centres as a source of equipment and ideas for teachers. The Ladbroke Centre, run by the ILEA, having been established for a great number of years, and having employed a large number of advisory teachers, is in the position of offering advice to others on the most effective way to help schools. A number of the mathematics centres are producing their own booklets on topics such as calculators, volume, games, which offer activities for the busy classteacher. Unfortunately most of the local publications are available only to personal callers.

A particularly useful publication of this type, originating from the Northants advisory teachers, entitled *Four Cubes* — suggests investigating the design of a house for Gnorman the Gnome using four cubes. The investigation requires plans to be drawn, wall paintings to be costed, gardens to be designed and costed, and the like. Even miniature people have to be designed to fit the garden. Although the children are not going to meet too many gnomes in their lives the exercise is fun and the mathematics readily extendable to real-life situations.

Commercial Schemes

The past ten years has seen an increase in the number of commercial schemes available for the junior age range. The introduction of colour enhances their appearance and makes them more appealing to children. Schemes with expendable workbooks have the advantage that the child concentrates on practising a mathematical concept rather than wasting time copying questions from a textbook. The schemes are not 'programmed' texts. The children will not learn by racing through the books. The teacher must teach a topic and then the children can be set to work in the workbooks for re-inforcement and to help the teacher appraise their own success. Most of the newer schemes emphasize the practical activities that are an essential part of mathematical understanding. Junior age children still require concrete evidence of the mathematical concept they are trying to grasp. In many instances the practical activities are not related to the child's own experience and it is the teacher's task to bridge the gap between textbook and personal experiences. Having mastered a concept the child should then be set a task which relates the concept to daily life, such as how many weeks pocket money are required to purchase a desired toy. So many texts or computer programs give 'shopping lists' that are unreal, an ice cream for 2p or a toy for 5p. The authors neither watch TV advertisements nor check prices in the shops.

The majority of commercial schemes now produce topic books that provide extension material for the more able child or can be used as source books of ideas for integrated topic work. The teachers' books are in most cases invaluable as a source of ideas for the busy class teacher. But no scheme is ever sufficient on its own. There will always be gaps. A useful book to have available is *Maths Links*[3] published by the NARE which lists the major published schemes and shows where related work can be found in each scheme. Care should be taken that adequate records of topic work are maintained for each child. In *Thunder and Lightnings*[4] (Mark, 1978) there is a delightful account of a new boy joining a class and being advised by one of his peers about topics. '"You could copy mine, only someone might recognize it. I've done that three times already." "Whatever for?" said Andrew. "Don't you get tired of it?" Victor shook his head and his hair. "That's only once a year. I did that two times at the junior school and now I'm doing that again", he said. "I do fish every time. Fish are easy. They're all the same shape".' Anyone contemplating the adoption of a new scheme would be well advised to refer to the discussion documents concerning this published by the Mathematical Association[5] and also to the review of modern schemes published by the Association of Teachers of Mathematics[6].

Mental Arithmetic

One area that is rather neglected by the commercial world is mental arithmetic but since the majority of junior classes these days are of mixed ability it would seem inappropriate to offer one quick mental exercise to the whole class, although I have one 8-year-old who can compute superbly mentally and is hopeless at written arithmetic. All children should be encouraged to develop their ability to calculate

Mathematics in the Junior Years

mentally and should discuss the various ways in which a correct solution can be found to a question, for example, 54−29 could be 54 − 30 + 1 or 50 − 29 + 4, etc. Plunkett[7] points out that any group asked to perform a similar mental computation will use a great variety of techniques and only rarely is the standard algorithm used on a mental picture of the sum.

Mistakes

Children need to be made aware that a calculation that is suitable mentally may not be appropriate when an algorithm is being used for a pencil and paper calculation. They should be encouraged to talk about their calculations whether the answer is right or wrong. I have seen a child after adding decimals check its own answers from the teacher's answer book and quite rightly tick each answer. When I asked what the decimal point stood for I was told the numbers one side of it were thousands and the numbers the other side just ordinary numbers. That one question revealed the child was lost, but a teacher might mistakenly have thought it understood perfectly.

It is doubtful if a child, whose mathematical learning is being fully extended, never makes a mistake. It is human nature to learn from mistakes and recent research has shown that children's mistakes in computation follow patterns which when discovered reveal a major lack of understanding of the algorithm being used. Although it is important for the teacher, when working with a group, to give positive incentive and immediate reinforcement by ticking the correct responses and querying the incorrect ones, it is nevertheless equally important to collect in the books later and study the mistakes made.

A query about a wrong answer often enables help to be given at the appropriate stage. An article by Newman[8] on division cites the following example: $8 \overline{)328}$ = 1216. When asked to explain Debra said 'Oh, that's easy Miss. You add the eight and three, put one down and carry one. Then you add the eight to the twelve and that makes twenty. Put two down and carry the nought. Eight and eight is sixteen — put that down too'. Debra was consistently mixing the divide and plus signs.

Similar patterns of errors are discussed by Ashlock[9] in *Error Patterns in Computation* and there are some examples below so that you can try your skill at spotting a child's error. It is interesting for teachers to make their own collections. But what matters is that teachers realize a tick or cross is not enough.

EXAMPLES:

Carol	46 + 3 13	18 + 30 48	8 + 16 15	42 + 56 98
Cheryl	32 − 16 16	245 − 137 112	524 − 298 374	135 − 67 182
Joe	27 × 4 168	34 × 6 304	45 × 7 495	

Ashlock also cites an American study of systematic errors in arithmetic which found that 67 per cent of children who made such errors whilst adding two digit numbers made a familiar mistake due to poor understanding of place value, viz:

$$\begin{array}{r} 88 \\ + 39 \\ \hline 1117 \end{array}$$

Children who have learned a wrong method are also capable of learning that they have been taught the wrong thing.

It is, in addition, important for all junior teachers to be made aware of the 'seven year difference' in attainment referred to by Cockcroft.[10] The fact that a task which an average 11-year-old can successfully complete, such as write down the number which is one more than 6399, cannot be done by some 14-year-olds but can be done by some 7-year-olds. It must also be remembered that many of the commercial schemes are designed for group work so that the wide range of ability in junior classes is catered for.

Subject Coordinators

The person on a school staff who has a post of responsibility for mathematics needs to be confident and enthusiastic about the subject and not someone promoted merely for long service. Cockcroft was quite specific about the role of the coordinator whose most important function was seen as providing support and guidance for colleagues. At the same time he or she should be aware that many teachers are diffident about teaching mathematics and will require a great deal of reassurance. In many instances it is practical help on the organization of a class into working groups that is required. The teachers who teach 'money' with never a coin in sight, time without time-keeping devices, and hundreds, tens and units without apparatus, are far more likely to be converted when they see materials being used successfully, than by any number of talks and lectures.

The production of supplementary material for both extremes of the ability spectrum is another practical activity that could be performed by the coordinator and may well be appreciated by colleagues.

It is hoped that forthcoming initiatives relating to INSET within individual schools will enhance the coordinator's prospects of improving the standard of mathematics teaching. If funds are to be made available to develop INSET within a school then hopefully cover will be available to enable a coordinator to work in a class with a colleague, or alternatively for another teacher to see the coordinator working successfully with their own class. There is nothing like a shared activity for improving confidence.

Another important duty of the coordinator is to ensure that an adequate supply of equipment is maintained, made available and fully utilized. This does not mean an Aladdin's cave of pristine equipment that is to be seen but not used. All junior classes require a wide range of materials and equipment relative to the needs of the children and these resources should be checked regularly so that quality is maintained. There should also be a supplementary store of equipment and a list of what is available throughout the school should be provided for every teacher so that they may borrow freely from colleagues but yet remain responsible for equipment issued to them. It is also important that a school has a consistent policy about the presentation of work in mathematics. Consensus must follow adequate discussion but the coordinator must see that any decisions are implemented. It is useful to have a sheet with examples of the layout used for various algorithms available on parents' evenings so that they too conform and do not confuse the pupils. The same applies to a school policy on the marking and correcting of children's work. It should be consistent.

Chris Bailey

Calculators

Not many farmers now use a horse-drawn plough. Few working windmills still exist and most canals carry pleasure boats rather then commercial loads. This is part of 'progress' and although a good case could be made for their preservation or even restoration it is a fact of life that they are all largely obsolete. It is equally a fact of life that small, solar powered calculators are relatively cheap and readily available, are here to stay and that cumbersome calculations are becoming obsolete. In fact research has shown that in some areas about half of third year junior children had their own calculators.[11]

Although many teachers fear that the introduction of calculators into the primary school will signal the demise of the algorithms of the four rules which inappropriately absorb so much of the junior aged child's mathematical energies, it must nevertheless be accepted that with the advent of pocket calculators the importance of algorithms is declining. Already many adults with the aid of a calculator will attempt more complex calculations than previously. Shopkeepers calculating VAT, for example.

In the junior classroom the teacher must consider the calculator as one of the tools of the trade. Mathematical horizons are being broadened by its use. No longer must examples 'work out' easily. Thanks to a calculator children can cope with awkward calculations quickly and accurately. Number patterns, such as digital root patterns, can be extended. Problems can be introduced which relate to the children's own experiences and can be developed from their own surveys and observations, thus dealing with real data and not oversimplified examples from books.

The calculator also enables children to concentrate on a mathematical concept without being hampered by complex calculations. What is the point of a child practising page after page of multiplication sums if at the end a child does not know what it means to multiply? Practice is quicker with a calculator and with appropriate discussion the concepts are readily understood. How often do children faced with a problem to solve, that is really just a calculation in words, ask 'is it add or take away?'. Faced with a tedious pen and paper calculation they are reluctant to try but with a calculator they are much more willing to experiment and to discover for themselves an acceptable solution.

There are many children with poor retention who never fully understand computational algorithms and consequently spend most of their time struggling ineffectively with 'sums'. In the end they become part of the adult population that hates mathematics. The calculator can change all that. It is a wonderful experience for a teacher to see an 11-year-old, who has never mastered basic computation, experiment with a calculator. To watch the look of disbelief and then joy when for the first time ever all his 'sums' are correct, is an experience not to be forgotten. The effect of continuous failure on a child's self-esteem is something of which all teachers should beware. A calculator can open a whole new world to such a child. Suddenly they can work on an equal footing with peers and their self-image is enhanced. The weakest child can keep up with the rest of the class at computation if he alone has a calculator!

All children should be encouraged to explore the calculator but need to be shown how to use it correctly, the correct order of operations and use of the memory, shown its limitations and shown the short cuts that are available. The calculator can be used to develop problem-solving activities through the use of everyday situations which formerly would have produced calculations that were too complex. For example, various 'mini-beasts' were collected on a nature walk and children wished to know which moved the fastest. In the past it would have been necessary to see how far each moved in ten seconds so that we only had to divide by ten to get their speed. The trouble was that some did not move for all of ten seconds whilst others travelled a very awkward distance like .53cms. With the calculator we can easily divide any distance by whatever number of seconds the mini-beasts move. The calculator can also be used to teach mathematical concepts, place value, for example. It can also act as a reinforcing agent enabling the child to repeat an activity many times over.

The Shell Centre for Mathematical Education at the University of Nottingham has produced an extensive series of worksheets on calculator activities for primary age children. At first sight these appear to be almost too much but in practice the children love them, Calculators enable them to progress at great speed. Teachers who have used them are most enthusiastic.

The Open University has produced an INSET pack for primary teachers and the publishers (Blackie) have produced a number of calculator activity books for the primary age group. Several of the published schemes also have topic books on calculator activities. Many of the teacher's centres are now producing their own collections of worksheets. Hounslow Mathematics Centre in particular has produced a very good booklet.

Chris Bailey

Computers

Most primary schools have one computer, several have more, few have a large bank of computers which would be the ideal but for the fact that the cost of the equipment, the cost of maintaining it and the cost of the software would be prohibitive. At that level of expense one has to consider whether or not the computer is a cost effective way of teaching.

In general I prefer to allocate equipment to classes for half-day periods as this minimizes the time wasted moving the computer and enables the teacher concerned to check that all is working well before the children arrive and the session starts.

There are so many programs available that appraising each, a lengthy business, is somewhat of a nightmare. Some authorities produce recommended lists of software and these are invaluable but the enormity of the task has forced many to abandon the attempt. Straker, writing in *Microcomputers in Primary Schools*,[12] provides a useful first list with a classification similar to that used for teaching styles in the Cockcroft Report.

Many programmes are designed to produce a specific skill and are useful as an introduction to the computer keyboard or of value to a less able child as a source of encouragement. In general these programs have little to offer mathematically to the junior child. Using the computer is often a stimulus in itself for the pupils but rather an expensive one.

There are a number of software packages that promote discussion and investigation. Several of the database programmes can be adapted for investigational work. Those which use the binary tree structure are a useful tool for classification. Others use a card index system which enables the children to create their own databases. An adventure game-maker will enable children to generate their own games, a pursuit which inevitably entails numerical planning.

Probably the most worthwhile mathematical experiences come from the use of Logo. It is a very useful mathematical tool since it involves not only graphics, either with a Floor Turtle or on the screen, but also programming. The children soon learn the commands for the graphics and are then able to generate their own problems. However, whether or not it is appropriate for junior age children to develop programming techniques beyond this level is still a matter for debate. As an introduction to this sort of work, many teachers find the INSET pack 'Posing and solving problems with Logo' produced by the MEP primary team in 1985 a useful starter.

Whilst some programs are suitable for group work and discussion most are best used by only two pupils at a time. The group doing practical work can have one pair on the computer, one pair tackling capacity, one pair doing practical measuring and so forth. All these activities need to be pursued most days by some of the class in order to give each child sufficient experience. Some time should be found when children can get hands-on experience in order to experiment and increase their confidence. It is here that a Computer Clubs often help. Whatever else, it is essential in all computer work that the teacher brings the group together to discuss their findings. Discussion of the program is essential and failure to do so reduces the activity to one of merely occupying children's time. There is no doubt that children enjoy using the computer and can quickly become even more competent than the teacher. However, the need is to remember that the computer is a device for improving mathematical learning and not simply an expensive toy.

Measures

It is important that practical measuring activities continue throughout the junior years. A link must be maintained between the water play of the infant children and the fourth year junior child's conceptualization of a millilitre. Without regular practical activities the bridges linking incedental measurements and more specific ones will not be built.

A useful strategy for bridge building is the use of five different colours to identify relationships, for example, five different containers marked with different coloured insulating tape for capacity, five different coloured parcels of different weights and five different coloured lengths of ribbon for length. Once an identification code is established then a progression can be developed. An example using capacity may help:

1 The use of five different coloured containers leads to ten statements of 'red holds more than ... ', variety and ten of 'yellow holds less than ... ' variety. (Beware — older juniors who have not had sufficient experience comparing the capacity of two containers will be unable to decide which of the two containers holds the most. Often they fill both to

the brim and don't know how to proceed.) Next, select ten sets of three different coloured containers and from these can be obtained ten questions relating to order, for example, red holds the most, yellow the least and blue is the middle one. It is interesting to allow the children to find the ten sets of three for themselves.

2 The next stage is to compare the containers with a standard but arbitrary measure, for example, 'red holds three cupfuls, blue holds five therefore blue holds two more cupfuls than red'. This again will generate a range of questions and the whole procedure can be extended by the use of a variety of arbitary measures.

3 The next stage requires the introduction of a set of related measures which can then be colour coded. There are a number of commercial sets of plastic measuring cones, cylinders or bottles that are ideal. Thence from the comparison will come the statements 'red and blue hold the same as yellow' or 'two reds hold the same as green'. A development from this is the introduction of formulae, for example, $r + b = y$.

   It is interesting to allow the children to discover these relationships and then set problems for their friends to solve.

4 Following on from this should come the introduction of standard measures, the litres and millilitres. First comes the estimation of which of two bottles/containers holds the most and then the measuring in millilitres and finally a statement saying by how many millilitres one exeeds the other.

5 There are numerous everyday experiences which relate to the concept of capacity and these should be used as the basis for problem solving activities. The dilution of squash, the purchase of petrol, wine, paint, weed killer will usually be part of most children's experiences. As Cockcroft[13] says 'All children need experience of applying the mathematics they are learning to familiar everyday situations'. At this stage it is important to remember that milk and beer are still bought in pints — sweets and greengroceries are bought in pounds and quarter-pounds. Not all measurements are metric and teachers must be aware of this. While Imperial measures are in daily use they are part of children's experience.

Mathematics in the Junior Years

One final reminder relating to measurement. As Cockcroft[14] says the 'ability to estimate is important not only in many kinds of employment but in the ordinary activities of adult life'. Realistic estimation should be part of all measurement activities. A boy told me he had won a race over 100 metres. He was asked how long it had taken. He thought it was between two and three minutes and was amazed when his teacher offered to beat that time.

Time

Research indicates that the majority of junior age children own digital watches. Shuard and Smith[15], found that among 500 third year junior children 61 per cent of girls and 80 per cent of boys had their own digital watches. In the light of this and having experienced the frustration of trying to sort out 'what the clock says' with a 10-year-old boy only to have him look at his watch and say, 'It's 11.40, good, only 20 minutes to lunch', it is clear that the emphasis in teaching junior children to tell the time should be on digital timing. After all we are expected to relate children's mathematical learning to their own experiences and theirs is a world of digital time and the 24-hour clock. There is plenty of material available free of charge to support class activities on time. Bus and train timetables are available from local stations. A set of last week's *TV Times* and *Radio Times* is usually available from the local newspaper distribution centre. Local travel agents are also a useful source of out of date timetables. All these are much more realistic and relevant than textbook examples. Whilst we still have the traditional clockface in classrooms and houses it is essential that the more traditional methods of telling the time should continue to be taught but we should now reverse the order of things and teach digital time first.

Multicultural Mathematics

There are many spurious attempts made by teachers to introduce a multicultural flavour into their teaching so that they can be seen to be reflecting modern day society. The end product is usually a potted history of mathematics with an inevitable bias towards western civilization. Does it really matter to a mathematician whether Newton or Leibnitz invented Calculus? We are just pleased to use it. Likewise did that marvellous figure nought come from India, China or South America? Again it doesn't matter, but thank heaven for it.

At the same time an approach from a different cultural background can provide the means of linking hitherto isolated work. Thus a table square reduced to digital roots and with say all the numbers six and eight joined by straight lines will produce patterns significant to Eastern cultures. Those patterns will vary with the choice of numbers. Again teachers can help children when teaching computation to be aware of the various methods of finger counting used by different ethnic groups. These are often very quick and efficient and are to be encouraged since even the most ill-equipped school has fingers readily to hand! It is also important for teachers to be aware of the various number systems used in other cultures. In different societies similar symbols have very different numerical values, for example the symbol 9 or something very similar occurs in Bengali, Punjabi, Hindi and Gujarati but takes the different values of 7, 1, 1 and 7 respectively. Thus, a child who appears unable to understand a concept is usually making mistakes by inadvertently reverting back to a previously learned number system. It is of course vitally important for all children that their mistakes are discussed so that any misconceptions can be put right.

Final Thoughts

At all stages of their mathematical learning children should be encouraged to talk about what they are doing. 'Whatever the type of response, there should be an analysis of the pupils' thinking even when the right answer is achieved. Pupils should be helped to find their own mistakes'.[16] In that way, they are encouraged to discover the faulty rule they have been applying.

As Cockcroft says, mental mathematics, which includes the oral work so vital to mathematical understanding as well as mental calculations already referred to, should form a major part of the mathematics taught in schools. Mathematical discussion in the classroom is vitally important since it offers opportunities for exploring and increasing the depth of understanding. This is an area sadly neglected in some classes where an individual learning scheme is used. 'In many situations in life oral communication predominates. It is therefore necessary from the beginning that pupils should talk about mathematical ideas'.[17]

It is a fact that lively mathematical discussions usually take place when children are carrying out their own investigations and are using mathematics as a tool for problem-solving and in exploring their environment. This is the nettle that junior teachers must grasp. Mathematical understanding comes from doing — from solving problems that are relevant and related to past experiences. The talk helps to sort out the ideas and develop logical thinking. 'It is essential that teachers should listen to any spontaneous comment from a child, and try to assess the degree of understanding revealed by it'.[18] Such discussion also helps the teacher to ensure that the problems set are not beyond the child's capabilities.

It seems to me that the future will see less pencil and paper mathematics and more discussion relating to problems to be solved. Since mathematics is a tool it must be used, for a tool that is not used soon becomes discarded. Too often children see arithmetic as a game with its own rules, an activity totally isolated from their world.

Finally, but probably the most important of all requirements, the children must enjoy mathematics. Once it becomes a trial and tribulation fear replaces reason, the rules replace understanding and the child 'switches off'. It is very hard indeed to win back a pupil that has taken this step.

Notes and References

1 COCKCROFT, WH (1982) *Report of the Committee of Enquiry into the Teaching of Mathematics in Schools: Mathematics Counts*, London, HMSO.
2 DEPARTMENT OF EDUCATION AND SCIENCE (1979) *Mathematics 5–11: A Handbook of Suggestions*, London, HMSO.
3 TURNBULL, J (1981) *Maths Links*, London, National Association for Remedial Education.
4 MARK, J (1978) *Thunder and Lightnings*, Harmondsworth, Puffin.
5 MATHEMATICAL ASSOCIATION (1986) *Six Discussion Papers: Choosing a Primary School Mathematics Textbook or Scheme*, London, Mathematical Association.
6 JEFFERY, B, STANFIELD-POTWOROSKI, J and MITCHELL-POTWOROSKI, C (1984) *Mathematics Teaching*, 108.
7 PLUNKETT, S (1979) 'Decomposition and all that rot', *Mathematics in School*, 18, 3.
8 NEWMAN, C (1985) 'How children divide', *Mathematics Teaching*, 112.
9 ASHLOCK, RB (1982) *Errors Patterns in Computation*, New York, Charles E Merrill.

10 COCKCROFT, WH (1982) *op cit*.
11 SHUARD, H and SMITH, DS (1985) 'Mathematics 6–13: An exploratory study', *SCDC Link*, summer.
12 STRAKER, A (1984) 'Microcomputers in primary schools', *MUSE Report*, 5.
13 COCKCROFT, WH (1982) *op cit*.
14 *Ibid*.
15 SHUARD, H and SMITH, DS (1985) *op cit*.
16 DEPARTMENT OF EDUCATION AND SCIENCE (1985) *Mathematics from 5 to 16: Curriculum Matters 3*, London, HMSO.
17 COCKCROFT, WH (1982) *op cit*.
18 DEPARTMENT OF EDUCATION AND SCIENCE (1979) *Mathematics 5–11: A Handbook of Suggestions*, London, HMSO.

Calculators and Computers

Brian Hughes

We devote a separate chapter to electronic calculators and computers because we believe that their increasing availability at low cost is of the greatest significance for the teaching of mathematics.[1]

The Cockcroft Report states that there are two fundamental matters to be considered. Firstly, the ways in which calculators and microcomputers can be used to assist and improve the teaching of mathematics. Secondly, the extent to which their availability should change the content of what is taught and the relative stress which is placed on different topics within the mathematics curriculum.

Calculators

In 1979, HM Inspectorate were already reminding teachers that electronic calculators would be with us for good, and that children then in schools would, throughout their adult lives, never be without a means of calculation at least as powerful as that available in the electronic calculator. They stressed the need for children to learn to use a calculator correctly and sensibly. 'If they do not learn to do this in school, where else will they learn it?'[2] In 1985 the Schools Curriculum Development Committee announced a major four-year project on primary mathematics, based at Homerton College under the Directorship of Hilary Shuard. An important part of its work was the consideration of the 'calculator-aware number curriculum'; the mathematical development of groups of children who have ready access to calculators was to be monitored over four years. In the same year, HM Inspectorate set out for discussion a framework within which each school might develop a mathematics programme appropriate to its own pupils[3]. One of the criteria for determining content was that account should be taken of the potential of electronic calculators, and one of the objectives for mathematics teaching was the sensible use of the calculator. The discussion paper stated that the emphasis in mathematics teaching could now be placed much more on conceptual structures and general strategies. The calculator is able to perform number operations but unable to give help in deciding which operation to use in a particular situation.

Dickson[4] and Shuard[5] are among many who have claimed that, with the availability of calculators, the emphasis in arithmetic teaching is likely to shift away from pencil-and-paper computation procedures towards the skills that are necessary to use a calculator effectively. The cheapness and availability of electronic calculators merely strengthens a pedagogical argument that has been in existence for many years. Adults appear to make little use of the computation procedures that they learnt at school, but employ idiosyncratic or common-sense methods. Research workers from the University of Bath[6] found that employees used a mental repeated addition method, rather than the paper-and-pencil long division procedure, when faced with the need to divide. Yorkshire Television and the Open University found the same repeated addition methods used when they asked people how many first class stamps could be bought for pound. Plunkett[7] wrote in 1979 that the advent of calculators freed teachers from the need to provide every citizen with methods of dealing with calculations of indefinite intelligibility; instead they should be introduced to methods more suited to their minds and purposes. Many are now arguing that children need to acquire good mental methods for doing the simple calculations often needed in everyday life, with a calculator being the sensible tool for more difficult calculations. Calculators are regarded as desirable aids to speed and accuracy in jobs which require a considerable amount of calculation and analysis of data[8]. However, the majority of young employees seen by the Cockcroft Committee to be using calculators at work had not been trained in their use either at school or on the job; calculators were frequently not being used in the most effective way.

Over a long period of time, reports concerned with mathematics teaching have noted that, whilst a high proportion of children in primary schools have been competent in performing calculations in the abstract, fewer have shown the ability to choose which opera-

Calculators and Computers

tions to use when given real problems to solve. The ability to perform number operations is of little use without the corresponding (and more important) ability to find the right operations for a particular problem. An emphasis on structures and general strategies is necessary if the ability solve real problems is to improve. In *Mathematics 5–16*[9], it is noted that evidence already exists to show that children's facility with number and their understanding of basic concepts will improve significantly if calculators are used *appropriately*. Nickels and Livingstone[10] describe many experiences, involving appropriate use of calculators, that they have had with children. They note the insight that teachers have been given into children's mathematical thinking, their misunderstandings and the strategies that they employ. We are, however, a long way from the situation where the majority of primary school teachers and their children are using calculators regularly or appropriately. It is a matter for concern that, with the introduction of microcomputers into primary schools in 1983, teachers were expected to learn how to use this new tool, when the majority of them had made little progress in the introduction of calculators into the curriculum. This has meant that in many cases the calculator has been passed by, its potential not realized, and its significance in mathematics education not understood.

A major reason for the very slow introduction of calculators into the curriculum between 1973, when the pocket calculator first appeared, and 1983, when the Department of Industry scheme put microcomputers into most schools, was the concern of teachers and parents that calculators presented a threat. Many have not understood the importance of mathematics teaching taking cognizance of changes in office technology and in home technology. A common view is that children have always learned a collection of pencil-and-paper computation techniques, so the same techniques must continue to be taught, without any consideration of the use or non-use of these techniques by adults. Some primary school teachers remain unsure of the mathematics that they are expected to teach; having struggled to find effective ways of teaching computation techniques, and being pressed to learn new teaching skills and content right across the primary curriculum, they cannot be expected on their own to find appropriate ways of incorporating calculators into their curriculum. Nor can teachers be expected to stop the teaching of some of the traditional computation methods when they see others continuing to teach them, and without any local or national decisions; recommendations such as 'some standard written methods of calculation, such as long division, should no longer be generally taught'[11] are on their own insufficient for the anxious teacher.

Calculators in the Existing Curriculum

In their teachers' manuals, new primary mathematics schemes are suggesting ways in which calculators can be used to assist and improve the teaching of mathematics. Some earlier schemes now have supplementary calculator material, but this can only be thought of as a temporary measure until the scheme is completely rewritten for the age of the calculator. Williams and Shuard have shown how calculators can be regarded as forms of structural apparatus to enhance children's understanding of how numbers behave. 'A simple four-function calculator can be sensibly used for exploration as soon a child knows the meanings of the signs +, − and =.'[12] There is no one perfect method for developing the understanding of a mathematical concept, and children respond in different ways to any one approach. The calculator is another resource that the teacher can use, alongside other resources, in the child's search for understanding. Calculators can also act as a link between structural apparatus and written calculations. As with all apparatus, talk and discussion are an essential part of the learning process.

There are many ways in which calculators can be used to reinforce children's grasp of elementary number bonds and to help to give children a feel for number, which is still one of the major aims of primary education. Most simple calculators can be used to count sets of two, or of any other number, by the use of the constant key. They can be used alongside number trays to reinforce and to check ideas about 4 + 5 or 5 + 4, for example, as well as for consideration of 9 − 4 and 4 − 9. If, through lack of understanding, a child writes 4 − 9 = 5 when using pencil and paper, it is not obvious to the child that anything is wrong; calculators would give an answer of −5, which could help the teacher in discussing the problem. Sets of flash cards containing simple 'sums' can be used as a race game, with one child using a calculator and the opponent using mental arithmetic for the same question. An important step in the understanding of tens and unit addition is the consideration of patterns such as 3 + 5, 13 + 5, 23 + 5, 33 + 5, etc.; traditional structural apparatus and simple home-made apparatus are still necessary for obtaining these patterns, but calculators can help children to

Calculators and Computers

see the whole sequence more quickly after they have begun to understand the ideas involved.

It is essential that all children gain an understanding of the concept of place value. Again calculators can be used alongside structural and other apparatus to help this understanding. Many examples of the 'space shooter' type of game have appeared in journals and teaching guides. A number such as 341 is entered into a calculator, and the three digits have to be 'shot away' separately, by the use of appropriate subtractions; for example the middle digit needs to be seen as '40' and not as '4'. Three hundred and one can be entered as 300 + 1 =, showing the form 301, compared with the incorrect form of 3001. Multiplication of a whole number by ten reinforces the idea of the digits moving to the left one place, with the units place being filled by a 'nought'. The Cockcroft Report[13] refers to the seven-year difference in achieving an understanding of place value which is sufficient to write down the number which is 1 more than 6399; could this gap be closed a little by giving children more experience with calculators?

Decimal fractions now occur in the use of money and of various measures; they are also likely to occur when quite young children use calculators for division. If they incorrectly enter 4 ÷ 2 = as 2 ÷ 4 =, the answer 0.5 appears. Division on a calculator does not lead to a remainder, so 5 ÷ 2 leads to 2.5, instead of the young child's answer of 2 remainder 1. Thus there are now many more opportunities for teachers to discuss the decimal point with children; a good example of such a discussion can be found in chapter 6 of the Open University course 'Calculators and the Mathematics Curriculum?'[14]. The sequence and timing of work on decimal fractions in the primary curriculum needs a major reconsideration.

Sometimes, however, the use of calculators may not be as straightforward as appears at first sight. It is often recommended that calculators be used in discussion of the results of dividing whole numbers by 10, 100, etc, as the reverse of the multiplication by ten noted in an earlier paragraph. There is, however, a problem here, because in most cases the decimal point moves whilst the digits remain in their original positions. In this instance, calculators do not record the result in the same way as a child would when using base ten blocks, so the use of calculators leads to the need for additional discussion.

Brian Hughes

The Effect of Calculators on the Mathematics Curriculum

So far I have considered the use of calculators in enhancing the existing mathematics curriculum. The main effect of calculators, however, should be on the choice of content for primary mathematics syllabuses, and on the relative stress on different topics within these syllabuses. Some consideration has already been given in this chapter to the need for a review of the teaching of methods of computation. The main emphasis will still have to be on a feel for number, on number bonds, and on place value; however, the use and understanding of a variety of mental arithmetic methods for relatively simple calculations will be more important than the ability to perform complex calculations with paper and pencil. Knowing *when* to multiply is at least as important as knowing *how* to multiply, the latter being of little use without the former.

The ability to give approximate answers by mental arithmetic methods should always have had a high priority, but it was usually neglected in favour of an emphasis on obtaining exact answers. Teachers who have been introducing calculators to older children have found that they are in difficulty when asked to approximate, because of their lack of early experience of this important technique. Quite young children should be encouraged to say that, for example, 12 + 19 is approximately 10 + 20, ie is approximately 30. Then, when they are older, they will more quickly see that 2341 + 1827 is approximately 2000 + 2000; children without early experiences of approximation tend to do obtain the exact answer with paper-and-pencil to check their calculator answer. This ability to approximate is an important part of the feel for numbers, and is now essential for predicting approximate results *before* using calculators to obtain a more accurate result. It should also help in the understanding of measurements as approximations.

In 1979, when electronic calculators were rare in primary schools, HM Inspectorate were already giving strong support to their use, and suggesting several forms of checking whether the user has made a mistake and reached a wrong answer.

> Does the size of the answer make sense?
> Repeat the calculation in a different order.
> Roughly approximate — for example, is the decimal point in the right place?
> Use of pattern (32 × 17 should end in 4).
> Check that the input data are reasonable.

Use the inverse process — for example, check a subtraction by adding.[15]

All of these checks apply equally to paper-and-pencil calculations, but the calculator allows teachers more time to develop the use of checks; for example, repeating a calculation in a different order was often tedious before calculators were available.

Teachers have frequently been advised to relate the teaching of number skills closely to the consideration of everyday problems. In 1978 HM Inspectorate[16] expressed the view that the effective application of skills including their use in practical activities was important, and that the teaching of skills in isolation did not produce the best results. Sometimes one of the difficulties of using the numbers that occurred in real problems was that children would be unable to perform the necessary calculations, despite being able to understand the situations. Calculators now enable children to overcome this difficulty, and the emphasis now shifts to the interpretation of the results. Calculators can give children confidence in their mathematics, and can help them to develop a range of trial and error methods, which will be useful to them as adults. For example, the problem of 'How many 17p stamps can I buy for £1?' might be solved by an adult thinking '20 × 5 = 100 ... 17 × 5 is 15 less than 100 ... the 15p will not buy another stamp ... 5 stamps and 15p change'. A child with a calculator could try 17 × 4, etc until they found the answer. They could then try 100 ÷ 17 =, and interpret the answer as '5 and a bit ... but I cannot buy part of a stamp ... 5 stamps and some change ... 5 stamps cost 17p × 5 ... (calculator) ... 85p ... 100 − 85 = 15 ... 5 stamps and 15 pence change'. When written down, these may appear to be cumbersome processes, yet these do represent the trains of thought described by adults when asked 'How did you do it?'. Teachers need to question adults about the processes they use, and to analyze carefully such trains of thought, before they can help children to develop similar skills. It also emphasizes the need for oral discussion of most of the arithmetic done by children. The lack of oral discussion between groups of pupils and the teacher is noticeable in some primary classrooms, and can be caused by poor organisation of mathematics learning and by too much reliance on written work based on printed materials.

Some secondary school mathematics courses have included consideration of accuracy, and of the need to interpret results. For example, when the edges of a rectangle are measured and the lengths recorded as 3.4cm and 6.7cm (to the nearest mm), how much reliance can be placed on the area calculated as 22.78cm^2? By considering 3.35 × 6.65 and 3.45 × 6.75, it can be seen that the area lies between 22.27cm^2 and 23.29cm^2. The tedium of doing two further calculations to find the bounds within which the area lay prevented full discussion of this, except when doing the exercise on accuracy! Pupils gave answers to questions in other exercises to more figures than was justified by the accuracy of the data. It is better that the pupil gives an answer such as 'The area lies between 22.2cm^2 and 23.3cm^2, whenever work with measurements is involved, rather than thinking that it has been calculated exactly. The same ideas should be important in primary schools. If two sticks with lengths about 4.7cm and 8.6cm are measured by a child as 5cm and 9cm, how much faith can we put in the answer of 14cm for the sum of the lengths? When the sticks are placed end to end, the child should record the length as 13cm! This can lead to some important discussion of the accuracy of measurement.

We have already seen that children using calculators will meet simple decimal fractions and negative numbers at an earlier age. They might also meet recurring decimals, square roots and reciprocals before they appear ready to understand these ideas. Recurring decimals, for example, involve the important mathematical concept of a limit. In 1972 Taback[17] found that even at the age of 12 only 20% of his sample could conceptualize ideas about limits. Does the use of calculators give children some of the experiences they need to understand this concept at an earlier age? How are teachers to react to young children who ask about recurring decimals? Questions of this type must be related to the statement made in *Mathematics 5–16* that 'as a general principle any move into new content should occur when the need for it has been made clear in the work being done by the pupils...'[18]. Teachers must think ahead so that they are not caught unawares when situations arise with calculators; whether or not they are already using them in their classrooms, children will certainly be bringing their own calculators into school and asking such questions.

Investigations and problem solving have developed in many primary schools over the last two decades. All recent primary school mathematics schemes include such activities, and much supplementary material is circulating locally and nationally. Many of the ideas involved are closely related to those discussed in previous paragraphs in this chapter. Number pattern work is a major part of many investigations; the speed with which children can use calculators to collect data helps in forming hypotheses and in testing these.

Whether the activity is a statistical one, a problem that is real to the children (such as planning a school trip), or a search for an 'abstract' number pattern, the calculator makes the task more manageable. The calculator allows teachers to use the investigative approach to learning much more than was previously possible.

Microcomputers

In the late 1970s, a few individual primary school teachers were using their own computers, together with programs they had written themselves, for drill and practice exercises and other limited uses in their classrooms. Around the country there were also a few groups, mainly based at colleges of education or teachers' centres, experimenting with other software for primary school pupils. The computers used were usually American, and a high proportion of the teachers involved were seen to be mathematicians. In the minds of many primary school teachers, computers were related particularly to mathematicians and to mathematics; computers were not for them! Little commercial software was available, and they did not like what they saw. In 1980, Seymour Papert's *Mindstorms — Children, Computers and Powerful Ideas*[19] was published in this country and stimulated teachers who read it. Without one of the few Logo implementations then available and the expensive computer on which to use it, Papert's ideas had to remain a dream for these teachers; the ideas, however, highlighted for them the poor quality of the software they had seen, and the lack of any stimulating educational purpose.

In their report in 1982, the Cockcroft Committee[20], having 'visited two primary schools which were known to possess micro computers', stated that there was an urgent need for programs to be written for use by children in the primary years, and that special attention should be paid to the development of programs for mathematical activities which would encourage problem solving and logical thinking in a mathematical context.

By 1985, as a result of the Microelectronics Education Programme, nearly all primary schools had at least one microcomputer, together with the experimental software in the Micro-Primer pack, first issued in 1983. As might be expected because of the speed of development, this pack was of very mixed quality and purpose. The Mathematical Association[21] expressed concern that some of the programs had serious mathematical deficiencies. Concern was also expressed that some of the programs used the new technology to develop skills that had been made redundant by this same technology. During the mid-1980s, however, a wide range of software has become available, including much that is appropriate for children's mathematical development.

These microcomputers have had varied effects in different primary schools and in different classrooms within a single primary school. In some schools, the use of computers has already made a major impact on the mathematics curriculum, and these schools are now ready to incorporate their use into their mathematical guidelines. In some schools, the only available computer has been used to good purpose in a limited number of classrooms. In many schools, however, the use is spasmodic, unrelated to the pupils' other work in mathematics, and with a lack of real educational purpose. Many reasons have led to this situation — the rushed induction programme, discontinuity in the availability of a computer in any one classroom, teachers' experiences with some of the early programs, lack of time to experience computer software, the use of published mathematics schemes by teachers without detailed preparation, and teachers' lack of confidence in mathematics teaching (with or without a computer). Straker and Blythe[22] have noted that the most successful primary schools have been selective in their use of software, reducing demands on the teachers while fostering progression and development for the pupils.

The remaining part of this chapter will consider possible good practice, but assumes the steadily increasing availability of microcomputers in every primary school classroom.

Microcomputers in the Existing Curriculum

Microcomputers are used with a variety of teaching styles. It may be helpful to relate this usage to 'certain elements which need to be present in successful mathematics teaching'[23].

Probably the most noticeable, and most frequently reported, aspect of pupils using microcomputers is the increase in *discussion* between the pupils, and the consequent development of mathematical language. This discussion appears to take place when using almost any software, although some is obviously more stimulating than others. The language and the understanding only develop fully, however, when the computer work is related to the pupils' other work in mathematics and when discussion also includes the teacher at appropriate times. Knowing when to join in and how to enhance the discussion is a new skill for many teachers to develop in mathematics teaching. A surprising number of teachers do this naturally in other curriculum areas, but have had little experience of it in mathematics. Some researchers have recently commented that these new skills developed by teachers using computers have later been observed in other aspects of their mathematics teaching.

There are many software packages which lead to *problem-solving* and to *investigation*, although some of the mathematical uses of these are not always immediately obvious. For example, a group of junior school pupils using *Flowers of Crystal*[24] as the basis of a project decided to investigate the probability of becoming lost in the fog on a particular stage of their journey. Over the past five years, Anita Straker and others have produced many computer programs that could give support to teachers who have little or no experience of investigation work with their pupils. Unfortunately many of these teachers still do not know of the existence of this software, because little of it was distributed directly to schools. On the other hand, well-informed schools have to make decisions about which software to use, too much variety being difficult for pupils and teachers alike! Good software may be used by a teacher to encourage the development of problem-solving skills, of logical thought processes, of sequencing, and of pattern finding in number and in shape; it may also be used to help pupils to apply their mathematical knowledge and skills to everyday situations. The most commonly used software packages within the problem solving category are now versions of Logo, which will be discussed later.

The microcomputer can be a powerful aid to *exposition* by the teacher when introducing or reinforcing a new idea, but this use really needs the availability of the computer at all times, or at least at very short notice. Graphics programs, for example, can be as helpful when used spontaneously to deal with an unexpected situation in a mathematics lesson, as when they are used in a pre-planned sequence of teaching. Here again, the teacher may be better advised to become thoroughly familiar with a small range of programs that can be used in a variety of situations, rather than trying to use too many different programs without the necessary familiarity with them.

There is no shortage of programs for the *practice of skills* by individual pupils or by pairs of pupils. Most of the early programs were of this type, many adding little to the pupils' mathematical experience, but, nevertheless encouraging some pupils who did not respond to the same approach from a text book, and giving immediate feedback on the correctness of the answers. Other examples in this category did use a games approach; they were an improvement on board games because they checked the pupils' responses and refused incorrect answers. Many of the number investigation programs make pupils practise a variety of number skills as they carry out the investigations. Good programs encourage mental arithmetic skills in a problem solving atmosphere, which also encourages the vital discussion between pupils.

The other 'element' listed in the Cockcroft Report is *appropriate practical work*. The computer is inappropriate for most practical work. Pupils must still observe, measure and record in real situations; they must use all their senses to explore the world around them. Watching objects apparently floating or sinking on a computer screen, for example, can never replace the pupil experimenting with a tub of water. Where the computer can be useful, however, is in the follow up of practical work — in tabulating, analyzing and graphing the results as well as in simulating further practical work. Many statistical experiments suffer, for example, from the tedium of tossing a coin enough times; after a pupil has looked at probabilities after 10 tosses, 50 tosses, 200 tosses, the computer can quickly simulate 1000, 5000, 1,000,000 tosses.

Microcomputers Changing the Curriculum

The concepts relating to number and to shape are independent of any software or hardware used by pupils in developing understanding of these concepts. However, the skills that these pupils must master change as technology changes. Papert[25] has shown how the fundamental concepts of mathematics can be understood and mastered by young children through the use of a Logo environment. Several versions of Logo are now available to primary schools, at very little cost.

Six facilities of Logo are turtle graphics, list processing, numerical operations, control, music and animated pictures using sprites. The turtle graphics facility of drawing pictures on a screen has been widely used in primary schools, often in a version of Logo that allows only this facility. Programmable toys have also been used, and some schools have controlled turtles with their computers. There is growing evidence that in the hands of good and enthusiastic teachers the introduction has been successful. Papert's philosophy of a child-centred education has led these teachers to encourage learning, partly independent of the teacher, through activity, investigation, and discussion. Infant and junior school pupils have developed mathematical concepts through programming in Logo. Other teachers must now be helped to give their pupils the right level of questioning and encouraging support within the Logo environment. They must have the time to experience the same environment before using it with pupils. It is not easy, in the short time often available within pre-service and in-service education, to give teachers this experience. If, however, they are 'taught' Logo then they are likely to 'teach' their pupils.

Structure and progression are needed, but not in a didactic manner; this is a new approach for many classroom teachers working with their pupils and for some advisers/trainers working with teachers. The use of the Logo language can be completely divorced from the original philosophy, and pupils can be trained to become efficient programmers, without gaining any insight into mathematical concepts. With previous innovations in mathematics teaching, the objectives relating to skills and concepts were usually clear to the initiators, but then become blurred. The potential of the Logo environment must not be destroyed by having a set of objectives concerned only with skills; teachers need to avoid the premature use of the proliferation of booklets with an over-structured approach to turtle graphics. Logo should be one part of the mathematics learning environment, and it has to be integrated into the mathematics curriculum, so some structure is necessary. For example, the development of the concept of angle will not be successful if approached only through Logo. On the other hand, the introduction to the concept may well occur at a younger age. The sequence of the development may well be different, 'turn' coming before 'corner', and 'exterior angles' coming before 'interior angles'.

The use of Logo can lead to ideas which are new to the primary school curriculum. A group of first school pupils 'realized that a polygon with many sides looked remarkably like a circle on the screen'[26]. This is an aspect of the concept of a limit; the more edges that are drawn, the nearer the polygon is to being a circle (ignoring the pixels on the screen!). Pupils using Logo have an introduction to algebra through using variables in their procedures. They soon find that it is more useful to have one procedure to draw a square of any specified size, rather than writing a new procedure every time a different size is needed.

Many teachers using Logo have had to convince pupils (and themselves!) that 'debugging' is a respectable part of mathematical learning. Previously pupils were told when their 'sums' were wrong, and often told where they were wrong. In working with turtle graphics, pupils should notice their own mistakes when the expected picture fails to appear on the screen. The pupils should find where the mistakes are in their programs, after suitable discussion with other pupils or with the teacher. Teachers have to consider carefully when to allow pupils to pursue a new objective for their drawing, because of a mistake in a procedure they have written, and when to insist on a correction of the procedure to achieve the original objective.

Full implementations of Logo have only recently become widely available, and it will be some time before there is sufficient evidence of the success or otherwise of the use of facilities other than turtle graphics. Pupils at present using turtle graphics in first schools may well need a full implementation of Logo if there is to be progression in their middle school education.

Database packages, with graphics extensions, have been developed for primary school use. Watson et al[27] have listed avilable packages. They note that databases help to concentrate pupils' minds on what data to collect, make it easy to enter and to amend data, and encourage multiple investigations from the data. These investigations were tedious when calculations had to be done by hand. Processing pupil surveys is an obvious use, but other uses in number, shape and statistics await research. Graph drawing from a survey can be very time consuming, but pupils must experience some for themselves. Once again it is the teacher's role to ensure that there is the right balance between pupil drawn graphs and computer produced ones.

Spreadsheet programs allow the display of data in the form of a table, and make it possible to explore the effects of changing variables in the table. Various groups, including the ATM, are exploring the potential of spreadsheets in mathmatics teaching. Milner, Peasey and Watson[28] have suggested that infant children could use them for counting, whilst ideas for data collection, simple patterns, tables, and sequences could be developed for juniors. A spreadsheet package may well become another multi-purpose tool in the primary school, along with a Logo package, a word processing package and a database package.

The emphasis so far in this chapter has been on the use of purchased software, either individual programs or multi-purpose packages. I have not suggested that teachers should write their own programs, and you may feel that I have ignored pupils programming the computer. Pupils using a Logo package are programming the computer, but are using a different language from the one they may use at home when programming their own computers. There has been much debate about the wisdom of primary school pupils writing programs in BASIC. Some LEA advisers have told their schools not to have pupils programming in BASIC, some teacher educators have argued that the programming language pupils use is important, whilst others feel that there are more important issues to discuss! After all, the 50 percent of third year junior boys who have a computer in the family[29] will almost all have tried to write a program in BASIC. A teacher in a Devon primary school was recently discussing the famous 'grains of rice on a chessboard' problem with her class of 9-year-olds. She was surprised that within a few minutes one of the class had written a short BASIC program to solve the problem; she could not have written it! The Mathematical Association has produced a disk of 132 short BASIC programs for use in secondary school mathematics lessons; several of these would be valuable in primary school investigations and the listings could be understood by many of the older primary pupils. Some would be appropriate for pupils to amend to do different tasks, and to enable the pupils to design a range of algorithms for a given task.

An issue that does need serious debate is the one of girls and computers[30]. Primary school teachers report little difference in attitude and ability between boys and girls; secondary school teachers report a very different story. If mathematics teaching is to make more use of microcomputers, we must ensure that girls are not placed at a disadvantage.

More consideration also needs to be given to the place of microcomputers in number work. Certainly the power of the computer, together with that of the calculator, emphasizes the need for different computation skills, as discussed earlier in this chapter. At the present time a microcomputer does have one advantage over a calculator — the whole of a calculation can be displayed on the screen at the same time — but this advantage may disappear as technology changes. The main advantage of the calculator is the number now available in many classrooms. Number manipulation has been present in most of the computer uses discussed in this chapter, but this does not imply that the computer is appropriate for the *introduction* of number concepts and skills.

Conclusion

Calculators and microcomputers are new technology in primary schools. They will not be used by all teachers all the time, nor should they be. What is important is the need to keep an open mind until much more research has been done and wider experience gained, to try them out whenever the opportunity arises, to use a small range of software packages initially, and gradually to integrate their usage into existing mathematics schemes. Only then can the implications for the future mathematics curriculum be debated in an informed manner.

Notes and References

1 COCKCROFT, WH (1982) *Report of the Committee of Enquiry into the Teaching of Mathematics in Schools: Mathematics Counts*, London, HMSO.
2 DEPARTMENT OF EDUCATION AND SCIENCE *Mathematics 5–11: A Handbook of Suggestions*, London, HMSO.
3 DEPARTMENT OF EDUCATION AND SCIENCE (1985) *Mathematics from 5 to 16*, London, HMSO.
4 DICKSON, L et al (1984) *Children Learning Mathematics*, London, Holt Education for the Schools Council.
5 SHUARD, H (1986) *Primary Mathematics Today and Tomorrow*, London, Longman.
6 UNIVERSITY OF BATH (1981) *Mathematics in Employment*, Bath, University of Bath.
7 PLUNKETT, S (1979) 'Decomposition and all that rot', *Mathematics in Schools*, 8, 3.
8 COCKCROFT, WH (1982) *op cit.*
9 DEPARTMENT OF EDUCATION AND SCIENCE (1985) *op cit.*
10 LIVINGSTONE, and NICKELS, (1985) *Practical Ways to Teach Mathematics*, London, Ward Lock Educational.
11 DEPARTMENT OF EDUCATION AND SCIENCE (1985) *op cit.*
12 WILLIAMS, E and SHUARD, H (1982) *Primary Mathematics Today — Third Edition for the Age of the Calculator*, London, Longman.
13 COCKCROFT, WH (1982) *op cit.*
14 OPEN UNIVERSITY (1982) *PM537 Calculators in the Primary School*, Milton Keynes, Open University.
15 DEPARTMENT OF EDUCATION AND SCIENCE (1979) *op cit.*
16 DEPARTMENT OF EDUCATION AND SCIENCE (1978) *Primary Education in England — A Survey by HM Inspectors of Schools*, London, HMSO.
17 ROSKOPF, MF (1978) *Children's Mathematical Concepts*, New York, Teachers College, Columbia University.
18 DEPARTMENT OF EDUCATION AND SCIENCE (1985) *op cit.*

19 PAPERT, S (1980) *Mindstorms — Children, Computers and Powerful Ideas*, New York, Harvester Press.
20 COCKCROFT, WH (1982) *op cit.*
21 MATHEMATICAL ASSOCIATION (1984) *Micro-Primer Software*, April 1984.
22 STRAKER, A and BLYTHE, K (1986) 'A primary overview: Part of the Mathematical Association's submission to the MEP critical review'.
23 COCKCROFT, WH *op cit.*
24 4 MATION SOFTWARE (1984) *Flowers of Crystal.*
25 PAPERT, S (1980) *op cit.*
26 TREADAWAY, M (1985) *Logo — Developments in Suffolk: Proceedings of the Logo and Mathematics Education Conference*, University of London Institute of Education.
27 WATSON, J et al (1985) *Some Suggestions for the Use of Databases in Primary Mathematics: Proceedings of the Mathematical Association's Primary Conference.*
28 MILNER, W, PEASEY, D and WATSON, J (1985) *Spread Sheets: Proceedings of the Mathematical Association's Primary Conference.*
29 STRAKER, A (1986) *Should Mary Have a Little Computer: Girls into Maths Can Go*, London, Holt Education.
30 *Ibid.*

Mathematics Resources in the Primary School

Jeffrey Goodwin

Introduction

We are all aware that you cannot teach without making use of resources of one kind or another. Whether it is a highly structured piece of equipment, a textbook or simply the classroom in which you work, all are resources and the way that a teacher and the children make use of them has implications for the style of teaching and the quality of learning that takes place. When considering resources it is easy to concentrate on the obvious, such as which textbooks or equipment to buy or make, but it is just as important to get the management of resources and facilities right if they are going to be used efficiently and effectively.

Consider the following situations:

Teacher working with a group when a child comes up with a textbook:
> Child: The book says get a box of shapes.
> Teacher: I can't get the shapes for you at the moment, leave that question and go on to the next one.

Teacher talking in the staffroom:

A funny thing happened with James, he recognizes five on the number frieze cards on the wall but when I asked him how many pencils there were on the table he couldn't tell me there were five!

Teacher to irate children:

I know that you and Shanta hadn't finished writing your

program to draw a house but Mrs Howe's class have got the computer today.

and

There aren't any more calculators left.

In teaching there is a compromise between what you would like to do and what you can do with the facilities and resources at your disposal. It is important to optimize this compromise by considering the resources needed, the way in which they are managed and how they are used with the children. Some situations can only be helped by more money, for instance insufficient computers or calculators; some are a matter of careful planning. If, for example, an activity calls for a box of shapes, they need to be easily available. Sometimes the nature of the material or equipment can inhibit children's understanding as in the case of James seeing five as a particular array on a frieze card.

It has to be acknowledged that teachers have many pressures on their time and would need to be super-human to anticipate every situation. It is, therefore, all the more important that careful consideration is given to the learning environment and the resources used in it, but what exactly constitutes resources?

The following list is the result of a brainstorming session and may be surprising in its breadth:

textbooks	measuring instruments
classroom	geometrical apparatus
workcards	television programmes
maths coordinator	radio programmes
advisory staff	posters
college of higher education staff	display space
parents	games
children	reading books
reference books	tape recorder
structured apparatus	sand and water
things from the environment	construction materials
home made apparatus	junk
booklets produced by groups of teachers	old magazines and catalogues
	off-cuts of fabric
calculator	overhead projector
computer	writing boards
consumables: paper, pencils, scissors, paint card etc.	professional journals
	storage facilities

sink
furniture
the environment
clock

time equipment
money equipment
gridded paper

and even this list is not complete!

The aim of this chapter is to consider the role and management of resources in the context of children learning mathematics. Thankfully, the decisions about resources are, on the whole, still left to individual schools. This allows for flexibility so that the resources can be the most suitable for the local situation and the needs of the curriculum. This makes it inappropriate to attempt to give definitive 'lists' of equipment. However, the points raised are intended to form a framework within which decisions can be made.

Buying Equipment

Have you ever been 'catalogue swooning'? I have page after glossy page of counters, sorting material, structured apparatus, shape and measuring equipment, games, puzzles, and so on, much of it a very useful addition to the classroom; yet how often do particular items end up unused in the cupboard? How can we go about making sensible choices and avoiding the point that a number of people are now making that for many children mathematics is plastic!

A few points of principle need to be established :

(i) The curriculum should come before the equipment. That is not to say that materials cannot suggest things. No curriculum should be that rigid, but when it is not financially possible to have everything then priority needs to be given to those items that are going to facilitate the teaching of the curriculum which has been agreed for the school.

(ii) Not everything needs to come from a catalogue. Teacher and child made materials can be more relevant and everyday items reflect the real world as well as being cheap.

(iii) Some things do need to come from a catalogue. Teachers have a limited amount of time and commercial production can do things that are not possible for the teacher. Who wants to try making their own Unifix!

(iv) If you are in a position to buy for the whole school, find out what your colleagues want and hence, will use.
(v) If you make substantial use of one or more commercial schemes make sure you have the resources to accompany it.
(vi) Try to see the item before you purchase it by visiting a mathematics or teachers' centre which has a display of equipment or even better, go to a school that is using it.
(vii) Remember VARM: Value for money, Attractiveness, Robustness and Motivation and remember that cheap is not necessarily a good buy. In fact it is often more economical to pay a little more especially when purchasing measuring or drawing equipment. It is also better for the children to use accurate equipment. Just think of the child trying to draw a circle with a pair of compasses with a loose joint.

The next question is 'how many should be bought?'. The truth is that if something is not easily accessible, and this may be because there is an insufficient number, it tends not to be used. The answer is dependant on a number of factors including the financial position, how much it costs, how important it is to have it and how it is going to be used. As a general rule if it is something that you anticipate will be regularly used in a classroom, such as counters, a tape measure or calculators, then there needs to be sufficient in the room for a child to use when the need arises, plus a supply, which may be in a particular classroom or a central store, when a class set is needed. Infrequently used items are best shared between classes but more than one set may be a good idea.

There never has been enough money to buy everything so planning over at least two years is a useful exercise, as is making a case to your local education authority mathematics or primary phase adviser for extra funds to finance a special purchase.

Everyday Items

Everything around us is mathematical and can be used to help children learn mathematics. You may think that this is taking things a bit too far so consider a few examples:

the classroom door for angles;
changing into plimsolls and counting the shoes in twos;

the pattern of bricks in a wall;
the shape of an egg;
a peal of church bells;
the number and colour of Smarties in a tube.

If we want to move away from everything being plastic then we need to use everyday items. As well as being just as flexible as the plastic they are usually cheaper and help to bring mathematics into the real world of the child.

Let me give you a flavour of the sort of materials I am thinking of:

cotton reels	paper clips
bottle tops	toy cars
bread tags	ribbon
pasta	sand
dog biscuits	water
conkers	straws
acorns	pine cones
shells	

All of these, and many more, are useful in a variety of ways and at a variety of levels for work associated with early number experiences, measuring, graphical representation, shape, statistics, etc. They will not replace the highly structured equipment such as Dienes apparatus or Logiblocs, or such things as plastic counters, but they will give a greater breadth of experience. As much as anything, using the things around us is a state of mind.

Written Materials

These can be divided broadly into two types: materials for the children and materials for the teacher.

When a school decides to purchase a commercial scheme it is investing a lot of money and care should be taken to evaluate the needs of the school and how far each scheme can meet them. There are many issues to consider and it is wise to view as wide a range as possible and select a short list. Talking to teachers who use the schemes and, if possible, seeing them in action are to be recommended. The pack *Choosing a Primary School Mathematics Textbook or Scheme* by the Mathematical Association[1] will prove invaluable.

The scheme will only meet some of your needs for written materials for the children, so you should also consider the place of reference books, investigation booklets, workcards you produce, instructions for games and the like. For all of these care should be taken in three areas: readability and use of language; gender stereotyping and a need to reflect our multicultural society. These are not always easy issues to address because they can have emotive overtones but deserve our attention all the same.

We should also not overlook the potential of mathematics from children's own books. For example *The Bad Tempered Ladybird*[2] with its concentration on time or *My Cat Likes to Hide in Boxes*[3] as a starting point for capacity and volume.

Written materials for teachers span a wide range but can be classified into four broad areas:

(i) Documents on policy produced by the school or local education authority.
(ii) Resource books which give practical classroom ideas linked with the philosophy that underlies them and which may well be linked to a particular scheme though the best ones are capable of standing alone.
(iii) Journals which share the current thinking and experiences of teachers and researchers. These may be particularly aimed at mathematics as is the case with the journals of the professional associations or they could be articles in publications which have a wider curriculum view such as *Child* or *Junior Education*.
(iv) Textbooks which discuss the psychology and philosophy of how children learn mathematics.

Of course, some materials fall under more than one heading and some will be more useful than others. A good idea is to display and make easily available those that have proved valuable.

Audio Visual Materials

If it were possible to spirit you into an empty Chinese restaurant, would you realize where you were? I suspect so, simply by looking at the pictures and the general decoration; even if you had never been inside a Chinese restaurant before. A classroom can do the same sort of thing. You get a feeling for the kind of things that are valued. If you want mathematics to be one of them it has to be represented on the wall and surface displays. Some of this will be the children's work and reports on their activities but you also need to consider items for the interest table such as objects with interesting shapes or examples of large numbers from newspapers. Wall posters can be a useful stimulus to generate discussion and investigation; some of these could be produced in the school and shared between classes whilst use could be made of the posters produced by groups of teachers under the auspices of the Mathematical Association and the Association of Teachers of Mathematics. There are also the many pictures to be found in magazines and periodicals, particularly in specialist publications such as *Child Education* and *Junior Education*. Have you thought of taking some photographs yourself?

The cassette player is now a familiar sight to most children. The spoken word which can be replayed if you do not understand or wish to rehear an instruction or piece of information is a powerful tool, especially as it can release the teacher for intensive work with other groups of children. The tapes can be ones that you or a group of colleagues make yourself or use can be made of the programmes that are being produced by the BBC, many of which are of ten minutes duration with written materials to accompany them. If you feel that you will need sets of headphones before you can use the medium try it without first. With careful positioning of the speaker you will probably find that it is not too intrusive.

Do not forget that cassette players can also record; a useful alternative to a written report of an investigation or activity. You may also like to try recording the children's discussion when you are not there or the more salutary experience of recording yourself!

The video cassette recorder has brought to an end the dilemma over how much some children were getting from watching a particular television programme at a specific time. We can now make better and more selective use of the broadcast material that is available and enjoy the opportunity of seeing something again. The ultimate, for the moment, in audio visual equipment is going to be the interactive video; a laser read disc, similar to the discs used on compact audio disc players, but which are computer controlled and allow an enormous amount of film, pictures and sound to be accessed. That is, of course, when the price is right.

New Technology

The three items of new technology which are having the most effect in our classrooms are the computer, the calculator and the digital

Mathematical Resources in the Primary School

watch. We need to come to terms with their availability, and hence, their use by our children in their everyday lives. Each presents us with a challenge to reassess our curriculum and teaching styles to take account of such powerful learning environments as the computer programming language LOGO or the understanding of number that the calculator can encourage in young children.

The calculator probably provides the greatest challenge to our present curriculum and the following should be noted:

> The electronic calculator is with us for good, and it is hard to believe that the children now in our schools will, throughout their adult lives, be without a means of calculation at least as powerful as that which is now available in the electronic calculator.[4]

> Calculators have become everyday tools in adult life, and the pencil-and-paper algorithms for the 'four rules' are disappearing fast; people now calculate mentally or use a calculator.[5]

Organizing Resources

No single structure for the organization of resources will work in all schools. However, there are some general principles which are worth bearing in mind:

(a) Each classroom needs sufficient of the materials that are used on a regular basis easily accessible to individual or groups of children.

(b) There needs to be easy access to class sets of equipment for particular occasions. These may be shared between two or more classes or kept in a central store. This is really to make the best use of the money available; it may not make sense to have six sets of Logiblocs in each of two classrooms.

(c) Everyone needs to be encouraged to return equipment promptly when it is finished with. If someone is continually using an item it is a good case for them to have their own set.

(d) Put some money aside for storage facilities. I suppose we should say put a lot of money aside, for the sort of facilities that are needed are not cheap. Easy access is essential and lots of cardboard boxes stacked on top of one another are not conducive to this. You may consider one of the systems of plastic boxes which hook onto a metal plate on the wall; where this has been introduced for the central store teachers have tended to make more use of the equipment.

(e) Storage in the classroom is also important. Again easy access, though this time for the children, needs to be considered. Make sure that the boxes or trays are at a suitable height and that equipment such as Unifix is not kept in one box but in a number of smaller boxes. Find space which is large enough to store equipment such as balances, when they are piled on top of each other they get damaged very easily.

(f) Written materials whether they are books, workcards, worksheets or games sometimes need 'preparing' before they are used. Covering with clear sticky film is often sufficient; a little attention before they are used can be very beneficial.

(g) Resources need maintenance. Sets of materials should be checked and if one set has a piece missing use it to replace lost parts of other sets; though experience tells me that it will be the same piece that is lost each time! Check for loose screws, torn boxes, smelly conkers etc. All children will be able to help to varying degrees and this provides a good context in which to discuss caring for things.

Group Work

The value of the class teacher being able to spend time with a small group is enormous. All children are not able to cope with the same concepts at the same time and need to progress at a rate which is appropriate to them, otherwise they tend to fail and develop that all too common malady, lack of confidence. The interaction within a group can encourage children to think mathematically and gives the teacher the opportunity to listen to the children and make decisions based on discussion. This must be one of the most powerful assessment tools that is available. However, a proper question that is often asked is, 'What do you do with the rest of the class when you want to work with a group?'

This is not the place to go into a debate on the various

approaches to classroom organization and the appropriate balance between individual, group and class teaching. For the experiences of one teacher refer to 'Making space for doing and talking with groups in a primary classroom' a chapter by Janette Warden in the Open University Reader *Developing Mathematical Thinking*[6]. There she discusses the way that she organizes for groups and gives a view of the social as well as the mathematical benefits. However, this *is* the right place to talk about the role that resources can play in facilitating group work.

First you need to do some 'consumer research' and make a note of what happens when you work with a group. Let us first consider those children who come up to you with a question. There seem to be three types of questions:

(i)   Please can I have/can I go ... ?
(ii) Please help me, I don't understand ... ?
(iii) What do I do, I've finished?

How you respond to these questions is going to depend on the age of the child but if you want to make the most of group work you need as few interruptions as possible. Let us consider the first question.

I suspect, but your findings will tell you, that the answer to 'please can I have ... ?' is 'yes, take one from ... '. Why not allow the children to take what they need when they need it? I know that there is the obvious danger of waste but if some time is spent discussing this it makes the children more aware of the things they use and encourages them to be better managers of materials; a benefit all round. Of course, some of the requests are for things like blocks or a ruler which you are only too pleased for them to have; all the more reason for them not interrupting you. For those pieces of equipment or materials which are valuable a special shelf can be used which needs your permission to visit. Interruptions are also minimized if things are easy to find. It is worth pointing out that you cannot change children's habits overnight and anything of this kind should be introduced carefully. As to 'please can I go ... ?' only you can decide on the extent to which children can leave your classroom without permission and this will depend on many factors.

The second question 'I don't understand ... '; children asking for help tempt us to give them attention and, of course, they need it. But at that moment and from the teacher? One of the best resources you have in the classroom is the children. I know that asking another child for help is sometimes looked on as cheating but is it really? Is it any different than asking you? Well yes, in that you may give a more helpful answer, although at times children do seem to understand their peers better[7]. The question could imply that the materials that the children are working with, be they structural apparatus or written, are not as useful as they might be. Materials need to keep children in a working context for long enough for them to gain from the activity and for you to spend time with others. The section on Initiating and Facilitating should be considered in this context. However, what if the child is stuck and remains stuck or is in the question 3 situation of having 'finished'?

This is a question of priority; is it better for you to concentrate on the group you are working with or break off and deal with the situation immediately. If you decide to stay with the group what does the child do? This again depends on the age and maturity of the child but even very young children are able to make some decisions on their own, that is, if they are aware of the alternatives. The important thing is to make your position clear, 'I do not want to be disturbed, look for something else to do from ... '. If you run an integrated day this may not be mathematical, if it is, it needs to be something which is ongoing such as a problem-solving activity or a short-term item such as a puzzle, game or investigation. From a resources point of view you need to have plenty of worthwhile materials readily available for these occassions.

Whatever you decide it should be remembered that fifteen minutes of concentrated discussion with a group is often better than fifteen seconds with an individual.

What about the children who do not attempt to see you but when you look up are either day-dreaming, talking about something other than the task in hand or generally messing about. Do not judge too quickly, we all take little breaks in concentration even when highly motivated. However, if the task is not holding them try some more 'consumer research':

(a) If there is written material, check that they can read and understand it
(b) Are they starting from a position of confidence?
(c) Are they practising something that they are already very proficient at?
(d) Do they have the right materials and equipment?
(e) Have they exhausted their span of concentration?

There are more questions that you could ask but all of them should be positive; except the last one which is, 'Are they being lazy?'. We are aware that some children are more 'industrious' than others and not all tasks can be scintillating but we can try to look carefully at the materials that we give to children and ensure as much as we possibly can that they are interesting and easy to follow or use. The section on buying equipment should be helpful.

Initiating and Facilitating

Some thought needs to be given to the way that particular resources and the manner in which they are used influence a child's learning. Children need to explore concrete situations and have the opportunity to talk about and come to an understanding of the underlying concepts. Very often in these situations the equipment or materials become a model for the situation, for example, counters standing for people. This is the resource helping to explain something that is concrete. The other approach is to have a particular skill in mind and use the resource to demonstrate it. These are not mutually exclusive but an over concentration on the second may lead children into thinking that mathematics is a series of tricks. There is the added danger, frequently pointed out, that the child may learn the apparatus rather than the concept and not be able to generalize the mathematics. Doing the same activity with different materials will help here.

Activities can be specifically designed to initiate thinking whether in the form of an investigation, a puzzle or a game. Games are often misunderstood; they can provide an opportunity to practice skills in an interesting way whilst encouraging a consideration of strategy and pattern. These type of activities are particularly useful for group work as, once they are set up, they require little intervention from the teacher; the difficulty is where to find them. Resource books of investigations are a valuable source as are packs of investigation cards which are available at times from some local authorities. I hesitate to mention any as they may well be out of print. A trip to your local mathematics or teachers' centre is called for or a letter to your mathematics adviser.

It is often the case that to gain the most from these activities you need a supply of consumables such as rough paper, printed papers with squares, or triangles, etc. for the activities involved are not always susceptible to neat recording in a book in the first instance. You will need to try them yourself to appreciate their value.

Jeffrey Goodwin

People

In many of the sections, reference has been made to mathematics and teachers' centres. They are excellent places to visit, not only because of the resources that they have on display or possibly available for loan but also because there is usually someone on hand to give advice. If you are not fortunate enough to have such a centre near you, there will probably be people available to visit your school to give advice and help. Contact your mathematics adviser in the first instance.

There are many other people upon whom you can draw as a resource, the most obvious being parents. They can form a valuable link between home and school and should be viewed as an asset in the classroom. I realize that there can be difficulties but the advantages nearly always outweigh them.

Conclusion

The purchase, management and use of resources should be taken very seriously if your curriculum is going to work successfully; but where do you start? One way is to organize a meeting of all the staff in the hall and tell them to bring all their resources for mathematics with them, everyone will be surprised by what happens.

Notes and Reference

1 MATHEMATICAL ASSOCIATION (1986) *Choosing a Primary School Mathematics Textbook or Scheme*, Leicester, Mathematical Association.
2 CARLE, E (1977) *The Bad Tempered Ladybird*, Harmondsworth, Puffin.
3 SUTTON, E (1973) *My Cat Likes to Hide in Boxes*, Harmondsworth, Puffin.
4 DEPARTMENT OF EDUCATION AND SCIENCE (1979) *Mathematics 5–11: A Handbook of Suggestions*, London, HMSO.
5 SHUARD, H (1986) *Primary Mathematics Today and Tomorrow*, London, Longmans.
6 FLOYD, A (Ed) (1981) *Developing Mathematical Thinking*, London, Addison-Wesley.
7 OPEN UNIVERSITY (1982) *EM235 Developing Mathematical Thinking*, Milton Keynes, Open University.

The Mathematics Adviser and Teacher Support

Richard Strong

Introduction

No matter how much effort an adviser puts into the support of teachers it is highly unlikely that either he/she or the teachers will feel that it is adequate. The balance between those issues which come upon the local education authority needing responses from advisers and the individual demands of teachers does mean that an adviser's time is at a premium. Priorities need to be established to ensure no area of work is omitted by neglect. That said, one of the major purposes of having an advisory service is to support teachers, no matter how that is perceived in each authority and by individual advisers.

From a personal perspective there appear to be three areas which need to be addressed when considering the 'mathematics adviser and teacher support'. They are:

(i) the establishment of a broad framework, in consultation with teachers and others, of areas where support is needed;
(ii) the establishment of the local authority's curriculum framework, with teachers, for good mathematics education. Teachers should then be in a better position to draw upon support services to enhance their classroom practice in line with that framework;
(iii) the management of the range of support services available to maximise their effect in helping teachers to work towards good practice.

Areas Where Support is Required

The support that teachers require is dependent upon their needs at the time. These will vary according to circumstances which can include:

(i) the stage of the teacher's career;
(ii) the responsibilities of the teacher;
(iii) his/her career aspirations;
(iv) his/her knowledge of new initiatives in the subject.

However teachers perceive their needs, they will invariably have in common the aim of improving practice in the classroom, the school or group of schools in an area. Issues will include the management of the mathematics curriculum. This will be by establishing and communicating good practice for mathematics teaching and learning, the management of personnel to achieve good practice, and consideration of the pedagogic aspects of mathematics education essential to the implementation of a sound mathematics curriculum in the classroom.

What follows in this section is a consideration of the areas where support is needed for teachers at varying stages of their career and later in this chapter links will be made to show how the local authority adviser can work in partnership to support teachers.

The Beginner

For teachers new to the profession their main concern is about survival in the classroom. Suddenly confronted with a class full of young children, the first priorities must be to establish good relationships; and create expectations for appropriate behaviour; and to secure organization in the classroom and the school. This is but a beginning. Before long the teacher has to be involved in teaching some mathematics. At this point she will draw on what she has learned at college and of necessity seek help from her colleagues.

The teacher new to the profession will need to seek advice and come to decisions on such issues as:

(i) the mathematics policies for the school:
(ii) how to organize the classroom for mathematics:
  (a) the physical layout of desks and resources;
  (b) the grouping of children;

(c) whether each group does mathematics at the same time;
(iii) the use of resources:
  (a) how to use the core texts;
  (b) what supplementary materials are available or required;
  (c) what apparatus is available;
  (d) how to organize the resources for ease of access;
  (e) what exercise books to use;
(iv) how to introduce and develop a new topic:
(v) how to match the mathematical tasks to the appropriate capabilities of the pupils:
(vi) establishing what records exist on previous mathematical experience:
(vii) deciding on a marking system and policy.

All of these issues need to be taken into account once mathematical experiences begin to happen in the classroom. Gradually over a period of time the teacher begins to gain a pattern of organization which fits her particular qualities and, hopefully, is consistent with the school's policy and ethos.

Mid-Career

There comes a time when a teacher needs to reassess her approaches to her own professional development in mathematics education. An organizational pattern will have been established in her classroom and the teacher will have many questions about mathematics teaching and learning which she requires to discuss with others; her colleagues, college staff and with local authority advisers. Furthermore, some teachers may have aspirations to become the Mathematics Coordinator in a school. Whether the motives are for personal interest or career enhancement there may well be a need at such a stage in a teacher's career to have the opportunity to learn about such matters as:

(i) coping with differing ages and ability levels in the same classroom;
(ii) the strengths and weaknesses of core texts;
(iii) stretching the able pupils;
(iv) supporting the slower learners;

- (v) providing a balance between whole class, group and individual work;
- (vi) developing and exchanging useful starting and extension activities for a topic to move out of the core texts;
- (vii) the place of the new technologies in mathematics education;
- (viii) using more open-ended enquiry type activities such as investigations or longer term projects;
- (ix) seeking alternative approaches to the teaching of particular topics.

These can be some of the most exciting times in the professional life of a teacher. Long enough in the classroom to feel secure and confident with children and colleagues; a whole range of challenges to be considered and worked at, and a career ahead which can be rewarding in the richness which teaching can offer. It is, therefore, important that eager and ambitious teachers should be offered every encouragement and support.

The Mathematics Coordinator

A further major area where support is required is for those teachers who have a responsibility for coordinating mathematics in the Primary School. At times these will be scale post holders, others will be deputies or the head. Each may need help to formulate a whole school policy for mathematics, a strategy for developing and implementing the policy and a programme for communicating that policy to staff, governors and parents. Amongst the issues to be considered will be:

- (i) aims for teaching mathematics;
- (ii) objectives to be achieved;
- (iii) teaching strategies to provide variety and balance;
- (iv) resourcing;
- (v) assessment and recording procedures;
- (vi) training of staff;
- (vii) evaluation of the curriculum;
- (viii) involvement with those other than the teachers in the school who have an interest and concern for the school.

The Mathematics Adviser and Teacher Support

Towards a Framework for Good Practice

A mathematics adviser will, as part of his activities, have to make judgments on the quality of mathematics education within a school. He will also be asked questions by teachers about what is considered good practice in the many aspects of mathematics education. It is, therefore, essential that the mathematics adviser should have some vision of good mathematics practice. It is also essential that the adviser is sufficiently flexible in his perception of good practice to make it possible to foster worthwhile initiatives. Teachers requiring support do need flexibility to develop their ideas but they also require a framework to put their ideas into a context.

One of the difficulties facing the education service in the 1960s and early 1970s was that there was no recognized opinion on good practice. Each adviser, each school and each teacher had the freedom to formulate and deliver their views and interpretations of good mathematics practice. The result was a diversity of practice, so much so that it became a matter of public concern in the early to mid-1970s. There was much confusion about what was meant by good practice. The popular press frequently reported poor educational performance and mathematics teaching was a regular feature of such articles. Teachers generally sought to combat this poor publicity but without much success. These were frustrating times because teachers were working hard to be efficient and effective but a consensus about good practice was lacking. Such a climate does not breed confidence and can lead to poor morale.

Research at the time highlighted four areas which primary school teachers expressed as being a problem in mathematics education. They were:

(i) *A Lack of Curriculum Planning*
There was little written evidence at an operational level, and frequently elsewhere, to demonstrate the setting out of clearly defined objectives. Generally, the mathematics curriculum was determined by a series of text books, and if topics were not included in the text or were covered inadequately, then there was no guarantee that these would be taught at all.

(ii) *A Lack of Planned Curriculum Continuity Between Teachers and Schools*
The continuity of mathematics curriculum was frequently interpreted as continuity with the next page of the book. There was little evidence of staff meetings to consider planned curriculum

continuity in any detail, although individual members of staff claimed to discuss these matters with other teachers in the school at the time of pupil transfer to another class.

(iii) *A Lack of Teacher Confidence*
There was no method by which teachers could assess whether or not their performance was adequate. Their goals had not been defined and therefore they were uncertain about what was expected of them, both in terms of what should be taught, and when, for the various ability and age groups. There was frequent referral, especially on the part of some heads, to the guidance offered by the 11+ system.

(iv) *A Confusion over New Materials Methods*
With much commercial influence in schools brought about by numerous series of new books and new teaching aids, teachers were generally confused about how to select materials and methods best suited to the needs of themselves and their pupils. Furthermore, the general impression given by teachers, at the time, was that in-service programmes had been difficult if not impossible to relate to their classroom practice.

These four general concerns indicated a need for:

(i)   help with curriculum planning;
(ii) encouraging discussions about mathematical development and teaching methods;
(iii) clarification of good practice in teaching mathematics and the heightening of awareness of the match between suitable mathematical experiences and pupil ability;
(iv) a means to help teachers select materials and methods.

The case for the mathematics adviser and teacher support was apparent. There was a clear case for individual advisers to react in a supportive manner each according to his personal interpretation of needs of the situation and in order to promote his own view of good practice. Herein lies a certain risk. With no national consensus on good practice advisers were left at the time to respond to or promote certain emphases in school mathematics. It has to be questioned whether or not it is reasonable to have, for example, two neighbouring local education authorities promoting different styles of learning through their mathematics advisers and how this affects, ultimately, what goes on in the classrooms.

By the mid to late 1970s there was a clearly recognized need to establish the nature of the state of mathematics education in our schools and to try to establish certain guidelines about what constitutes good practice in mathematics education. Any national initiative was likely to be viewed with some suspicion for fear that what might emerge would be imposed and at odds with a teacher's own practice. There would also be fears that there would be no place for the initiative and freedom for teachers so cherished by the profession. From the anxieties of the past decade have emerged a series of enquiries, surveys and reports, including the national surveys at primary, first and middle school level; the national surveys of the Assessment and Performance Unit; the *Enquiry into the Teaching of Mathematics* by the Cockcroft Committee; *Mathematics 5–11* and *Mathematics 5–16* from HMI and DES enquiries into the curricular policies of local education authorities.

These national surveys and suggestions, far from being restrictive, have in fact offered a sound and professional base from which the teaching of mathematics in the primary school can be considered for the next decade forward. There is much still to be considered; the effect of new technologies, making mathematics more relevant, doing mathematics which encourages mathematical thinking and new initiatives in assessment, but stock has been taken of the state of the art and some ground rules established which try to define good practice.

The Problem

The difficulty which mathematics advisers now face is to formulate modes of operation which bring together in a realistic manner the ideas in the reports and surveys with activities which take place in classrooms. Here each adviser has to provide the interface. There is no guarantee that every primary school teacher will have read the reports and surveys and, more importantly, put some of their ideas into practice. With primary teachers having to teach a wide range of subjects to children of a wide range of ability it is unrealistic for them to comprehend current thinking in all curriculum areas without the support of other professional colleagues. It is in such a situation that the mathematics adviser has to comprehend and interpret in an unbiased manner the national messages about good mathematics practice and communicate them to whole staffs and individual teachers in many schools according to their unique needs and particular stages of development.

Richard Strong

At no stage in the past twenty-five plus years, when prior to this the approach to teaching mathematics was almost certainly mechanical and the style authoritarian, have mathematics educationists and primary school teachers had so much evidence and clearly expressed documentation about what constitutes current thinking about good practice. Much that has emerged has been acclaimed as sound and realistic and yet setting challenges for classroom practice. It is hoped that the responsibility of each mathematics adviser, together with the primary school teachers is to offer a vision of good practice in primary mathematics and to establish what means to use to support teachers in their search for improvements in classroom practice which are in line with the broad frameworks of national trends. But how might such a framework of support be defined and be recognized and at the same time allow for flexibility within it?

A Curriculum Framework for Support in Mathematics Education

If it is accepted that the mathematics adviser should as part of his role act as an interface between national messages and classroom practice in support of teachers, then for any of the adviser's arguments and longer term planning to have any coherence he/she must have a curriculum model which acts as his/her expression of good practice and as a vehicle for communication.

Such a model which has been found useful is shown below:

Figure 1 A mathematics curriculum model

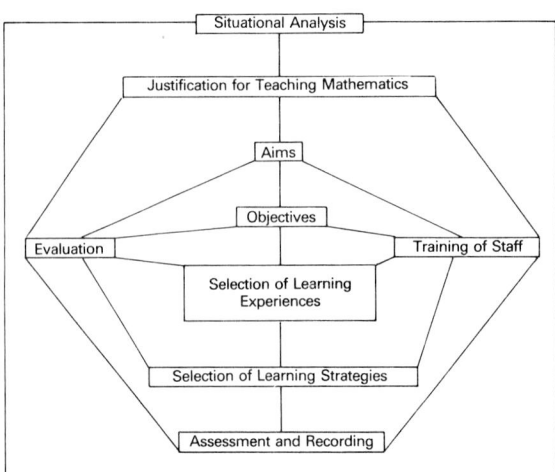

The Mathematics Adviser and Teacher Support

The overall model offers shape to curriculum development and allows teachers to recognize the component elements of a mathematics curriculum. Working groups of teachers on courses have been able to bring their expertise to the development and enhancement of various parts of the model so that it is never static and always totally involves teachers working with the mathematics adviser and, frequently, staff from higher education.

Such an approach was recognized by local teachers to give the real and necessary support they required in the light of their expressed concerns during and immediately after the publicity on accountability in education of the early to mid-1970s. The aim of such action was to offer a plan of action and level of involvement which offered a sense of purpose and direction with the resultant effect of raising awareness and confidence amongst those involved in primary mathematics within a local education authority.

With the HMI survey, Cockcroft Report and APU studies the objectives of good mathematics teaching have been broadened for the better. These objectives include a need to raise the awareness and status of:

(i) general problem solving strategies which includes investigations (these strategies are often referred to as the 'processes' involved in doing mathematics);
(ii) using mathematics in context;
(iii) personal qualities of pupils through mathematics which are in keeping with the general aims of the school.

It has been recognized that traditionally too many pupils have been offered mathematical content (concepts, knowledge and skills) with which they only met with failure. It has been suggested that many pupils should do less mathematics (content) and would be more successful. Such a move would create the opportunity for the broadening of objectives described above. The issue facing mathematics advisers in their support of teachers is how to help teachers achieve these broad objectives through less mathematics content. Without a convenor, catalyst, intervenor or whatever, there is a real danger that the recent and valuable redefinition of mathematics education will merely gather dust.

To be specific, in a local sense, current national ideas and recommendations have helped clarify the mathematics curriculum model shown earlier at a time when one local authority was at a stage of readiness for further work in mathematical support. Several teachers and the mathematics adviser were seeking to enrich the mathematical diet of pupils by encouraging work away from the core text and also to create more worthwhile opportunities for developing mathematical thinking and real understanding. At the time of development of the model (noted above) these process orientated aspects of education were not the focus of attention, at least locally, and indeed in the mid-seventies no clear consensus about them existed.

The result of the new consensus is that the objectives of mathematics education have been broadened. The teaching styles and learning strategies have been more clearly expressed to encourage a broader range of approaches and activities. Greater awareness is being made of the need for different styles of mathematical resources to get away from the predominance of text book style learning and to provide opportunities for developing a more practical, enquiring and open approach to learning. The mathematics adviser has at the local level the task of helping to encourage such actions. Without that support teachers and school staffs as a whole will have to react in isolation and that will be a less rich mathematical experience for the children than if views are shared with others. The value of the local mathematics curriculum model may well not be in its degree of rightness or wrongness but in the quality of the discussion which it engenders.

In summary, central to the mathematics adviser and teacher support is the issue of providing leadership at the interface between national recommendations for good practice and events in classrooms. Teachers need to have a clear vision of what constitutes good mathematics practice. A report can state the component parts but their enactment in classrooms requires translating them into a locally understood framework. The adviser having a framework, being able to communicate and develop his views with teachers, is one important aspect of teacher support. What follows describes a range of advisory activities which support teachers either individually or as a whole staff or area cluster, each according to their needs and within the context of the curricular model which should be all-embracing.

The Mathematics Adviser and Teacher Support

Vehicles for Providing Support

One of the major challenges of a mathematics adviser is to try to meet and support the needs of teachers whose demands vary enormously. There is a danger of responding to demands in a one-off, piecemeal fashion which may solve a short-term problem — and at times that will be necessary — but fail to have any longer-term benefits. It has to be recognized that if support is about managing change for the improvement of teaching then there are few, if any, short term solutions. Furthermore, no adviser can work in isolation from teachers' views. At times teachers will nudge the adviser into action because he has failed to recognize or react to a need and at other times the adviser will nudge a school into action, and if the professional relationship is 'right' the interaction and experiences gained can be very rewarding. Equally, no adviser can operate fully without working closely with colleagues from higher education or the Inspectorate since they have a wealth of expertise and experience to bring to and share with those working in local authorities.

It is important that a mathematics adviser has, at least in his mind's eye, some idea of the parameters which might govern the framework of supportive activities for teachers. The following represent some classifications:

In-Service Courses	Resource Centre
Working Groups	Support Staff
In-School Support	Information Flow

In-Service Courses

It is not always appreciated just how expensive it is to provide in-service and finance is frequently a determining factor in the amount and type of in-service available. Furthermore, often the only way to obtain funding is to adhere to externally set conditions about duration and qualification for participation. So it must be recognised that advisers' plans for delivering in-service provision are limited. That stated, how might a broad programme for in-service be considered?

Teacher initiated It is essential to support the needs of individuals or groups of teachers when they have recognized issues of value to them. The motives can vary. They may be for self-centred reasons or for a perceived school need. In the case of the former many primary teachers want in-service to better understand the nature of the issues about good mathematics teaching and their sole aim is to improve the quality of performance in their own classroom. Others have the added incentive of increasing promotional prospects. The last reason may encompass a whole school need — the staff of a school frequently decides to concentrate on a particular area of the curriculum through one member of staff being up-dated on current views of good practice.

The mathematics adviser needs to be able to respond to such demands. At times this will mean advising on particular courses being offered in higher education or offering a course within the authority or at times providing support in the school.

Teacher 'persuaded' The term 'persuade' conjures up many unfortunate images and one can only hope that the reader will recognize the need for its use by reading on. There are at times those teachers whose performance in a particular area of their work could be improved. If they have not initiated help themselves then, rather than allowing them to become a matter of concern, it is to the benefit of the individual teacher (and the school) that help and support should be given with a view to raising the level of performance to an acceptable level.

There are also those teachers whose work is quite excellent who need to be 'persuaded' that they have something to pass to others and therefore need time out of school to develop their ideas. There are many such people whose talents never emerge and yet they have qualities from which we can all learn.

Adviser initiated These are the courses which the adviser will promote either because of his/her recognition of a need across the local authority, such as training of primary mathematics coordinators, or to raise awareness and understanding of issues being considered nationally. Teachers need to be made aware of whether these courses are 'one-offs' or 'ongoing' so that they can plan their attendance. All too often courses occur in a piecemeal fashion and teachers find it difficult to plan for their longer term professional development.

Another useful adviser initiated action is for a teacher to be given the opportunity to visit another school. Teachers seldom have this opportunity and yet it is a very rich form of in-service education.

The Mathematics Adviser and Teacher Support

Working Groups

Working groups usually spearhead the activities in the author's authority. Teachers join them by invitation and recommendation. The in-service element of a working group is enormous because of the discussions involved. It is important with such groups that they bring in new people each time and to try to have a wide representation of backgrounds and views.

Locally these groups have formulated the mathematics curriculum model and then brought it nearer to the classroom by providing exemplars of various styles of teaching. Over recent years such groups have been of key importance in working with the mathematics adviser to provide exemplars of:

   (i)   extension material for able pupils;
   (ii) support materials for slow learners;
   (iii) more open style, not content specific, mathematical investigations;
   (iv) supplementary materials to enrich and support the learning of particular topics;
   (v)   cross-curriculur or unified topic work involving mathematics;
   (vi) materials for parent links;
   (vii) and others.

These exemplars are then offered to other teachers in the authority through in-service work and school visits.

In-School Support

Although, in principle, when an individual teacher returns to her school from a course there ought to be a gain for the whole staff, in practice, unless the teacher is well supported by the head and other colleagues and encouraged to feed back ideas into the school, many of the ideas from the course will not reach other staff. An advantage of teachers attending courses is that they are meeting and sharing ideas with others. Course providers do need, however, to ensure that what takes place on the course does relate to what happens in the school. It is helpful if mechanisms can be established whereby the teacher on the course can get colleagues in her school involved in activities from the course — perhaps trialling of materials, or team teaching a new piece of work.

Richard Strong

Frequently schools require support which is specific to their needs as a staff and for which a course is not really suitable. Such provision is heavy on support service time but very rewarding in result. They can take the form of evening meetings or school closure for in-service days or working with the teachers in their classrooms. Locally, the latter provision has been enhanced by the very valuable resource of primary support teachers for mathematics, whose prime purpose is to work in classrooms with teachers.

Another valuable in-school support — although if conducted insensitively it can create problems — is an external evaluation of the mathematics in the school. Advisers are very aware of a range of primary practices across many schools and should therefore be in a position to bring to the notice of teachers their strengths and weaknesses. By open and frank discussions leading to development plans, such visits and their ensuing action can be a rich form of teacher support.

Resource Centre for Mathematics

Teachers are always searching for new ideas and materials and therefore the greater the range of resources which can be brought to their attention, the better. Such resources, if not to be overwhelming, need to be carefully referenced by a system which operates in the teachers' interests. For example, a teacher might be introducing a new content area and therefore need to reference, by a specific content heading, interesting practical starting points and consolidation materials. The referencing system needs to have such help readily available rather than expect a teacher, perhaps in an after-school visit, to have to search through numerous resources in the hope of finding something suitable.

Teachers will also, at times, need to review core texts and apparatus and it is valuable and a financial saving to them if materials are available at a central point. Additionally, such a central point can become a focal point for information and in-service work requiring resources on the spot.

Support Staff

There appear to be several levels of support as curriculum development is currently considered. There is research, committees and enquiries which shape national reports, offer consensus views on the state of the art of mathematics education, and make recommendations. The local education authorities have to shape their own curricular policies, taking into account national messages and local situations. This will mean establishing, amongst other things, curricular frameworks for good practice. Schools then have to translate these frameworks into school policies and teachers have to make these policies operational in the classroom.

National reports, local education authority curriculum frameworks for mathematics and daily classroom activities can be a long way removed from each other, and unless bringing the two extremes together is carefully managed, they could easily bear little relationship to each other. Reports need to be much more than words on a page having meaning only to the authors. Phrases such as 'getting the child more involved in the learning process'; 'general problem solving strategies'; 'investigations and investigational approaches'; 'holistic approaches'; need to be clarified. They can be confusing unless teachers can relate them to activities in their own classrooms.

Locally, one of the most valuable teacher support services available is the employment of advisory teachers through the educational support grant and primary support teachers through a local education authority. The former are initially working with teachers to provide classroom activities as exemplars to give meaning to words in reports and curriculum frameworks. When they have a bank of such activities, trialled in schools, to demonstrate balance in teaching and learning styles and aproaches, then much of their work will be school-based or school-focussed to introduce the ideas into schools. Primary support teachers spend most of their time working in classrooms with children actually using materials to promote certain styles of learning as the exemplars become available or responding to specific needs of teachers and yet still attempting to encourage a local education authority's code of good practice.

It is the aim that, over a period of time, such a planned approach will bring a coherence to national, local authority and school activity.

Information Flow

To have a back-up support service for teachers which can include county advisers, advisory teachers, primary support teachers, resource centre[5], in-service courses, working groups and a curriculum framework for mathematics and not keep teachers well informed of this support would do a disservice to all concerned with mathematics education in a local authority. It is therefore essential that teachers should know of and be kept up-dated with information about which exists to help them.

Summary

This chapter represents a personal view of the topic 'The mathematics adviser and teacher support'. There will probably be as many approaches to the topic as there are mathematics advisers. From this article, however, readers should be better informed about some of the issues involved, viz:

(i) determining where support is needed;
(ii) determining a curriculum framework so that those involved in mathematics education can at any stage recognize their particular development in the context of a cohesive whole;
(iii) managing the range of support activities for the maximum benefit of teachers and, ultimately, children.

Assessment and Evaluation

Peter Whitfield

If teaching is to be successful, it is essential that the teacher should assess what is happening.[1]

In many schools today a situation exists where a great deal of thought has gone into planning a curriculum which is seen as relevant to the needs of the children and to the needs of society. After much staff discussion, policies on content, method and recording have been agreed. The teachers cooperate fully and enthusiastically in implementing these agreed ideas. However, although the staff fully believe they have devised the best possible teaching and learning situation for the children they still, at the end of the day, are faced with the question, 'How do we know that our ideas are working?'. This is a real and crucial problem, even in the most favourable set of circumstances.

It would seem sensible, at this point, to examine the two terms 'assessment' and 'evaluation'. The terms are commonly used together as if they were identical and certainly the dictionary definitions would suggest that there is indeed very little difference between them. In educational terminology, though, the difference in meaning is rather important. The term 'assessment' has come to be regarded as being involved in setting a value on a pupil's performance; his actual achievement, the process used by the pupil and his attitudes towards mathematics. Assessment enables the teacher to make a statement about the individuals in receipt of education. 'Evaluation' by contrast has come to be used in making judgments on the actual education being provided; on the suitability of the curriculum and syllabus and how appropriate and effective the teaching is. Evaluation examines educational provision. So we assess pupils and evaluate curricula.

Peter Whitfield

The introductory quotation raises the point of teachers being successful. The assumption is that teachers are actively interested in assessment of their work. Probably the majority are, simply because it is the surest route by which a teacher can appraise his/her own work and then search for ways to improve it. This is a constant aim of a good teacher.

Assessment Evaluation and Teaching

Assessment is important in helping a teacher to be successful. What are the features of assessment which make it essential? Several points can be considered to clarify the links between assessment and good teaching.

Assessment can take various forms but common to them all is the fact that in assessing, the teacher will consider how best children learn. Account will be taken of whether what is offered to children in the way of learning experience is suitable to their needs and will indeed enable them to learn in the ways considered best by any particular school. That is, is the teaching appropriate?

Assessment leads the teacher to examine and sharpen her knowledge of how children acquire mathematical concepts; what will retard or damage acquistion of them; progression in acquiring concepts; and the mathematical environment being provided in the classroom.

The mathematical environment provided is largely a reflection of the teachers' attitudes towards mathematics. In examining his/her own attitudes the teacher will consider whether the activities are stimulating and interesting; whether a wide mathematics curriculum is being provided. Also, very important is the provision of opportunities which will foster good teacher/pupil relationships so that discussion will be an integral part of the mathematical climate. Above all the teacher's attitude should encourage and demonstrate to children that mathematics is enjoyable and interesting and is to be found in every aspect of their everyday lives. The link between the teachers' and pupils' attitudes is accepted. Even where assessment is informal — it may simply take the form of observation by the teacher — the extent to which it affects children's attitudes is considerable. Children gain some idea of levels to be attained. Important guidance on poor or faulty concept acquisition or application can be assimilated quite easily. The pupil will gain from knowledge that concepts have been correctly acquired and applied. The pupil becomes aware that his individual progress, or lack of it, is of concern to the teacher. So assessment has a direct bearing on the attitudes of both teacher and pupils.

The teacher has to examine more than his/her day-to-day teaching. He/she has to consider the wider issue of whether the curriculum being offered 'matches' his/her expectations of pupil acquisition of mathematics. A common curriculum is not needed but the teacher must have his/her own broad framework within the school's agreed aims and objectives. The content of the mathematics curriculum which the teacher provides must be such that both his/her aims and those of the school can be fulfilled. Evaluation of this kind should be an integral part of the teacher's responsibility towards his/her pupils. The question may arise as to the suitability of what is being offered; is it answering the children's needs? has a sensible age match been made with certain mathematical concepts? is the order of concepts to be acquired correct? It is obvious that the mathematics curriculum within a school will not remain a stagnant entity. It should often be reviewed and adapted to changing needs and technology. Evaluation of the curriculum ensures that the teachers remain positive rather than indifferent about their teaching.

Assessment and evaluation infers that there is a set of agreed aims and objectives within a school. These give the teacher a basis upon which to decide what and how he/she is to teach. This being so it can be seen that assessment will give an indication of the effectiveness of the teaching within both the school as a whole and in individual classes. Through assessment the teacher will be able to decide on what is the most suitable activity for each individual in his/her class. She will know whether a change of direction is needed or whether reinforcement of work already covered is the best course of action. Such decisions can be made readily only where assessment takes place. The teacher's knowledge and intuition are not devalued by assessment. Teachers often need something more tangible than intuition when they feel a change of direction may be necessary. Teaching becomes more effective when assessment is part of the teacher's armoury.

The class teacher usually has a good understanding of how his/her pupils are progressing, but this intuition is not infallible and most teachers would admit that this is so. Most classes in primary schools are mixed ability classes, usually with a wide ability range. It is imperative then that the teacher knows what is appropriate for each individual. Assessment takes various forms and the type used will be governed by what the teacher needs to know at any given time. Assessment can simply give teachers knowledge about their pupils' achievements or, in the case of diagnostic assessment, it can identify a pupil's difficulties.

Different Types of Assessment

Assessment or testing carried out by teachers can be either formal or informal but care must be taken to ensure that the teacher is actually testing what he/she means to test. Compiling tests is a difficult task and much has to be considered. Tests may prove that only a particular area of knowledge has been learned, for example, number bonds, multiplication or tables. Whether or not real understanding of addition or multiplication has been acquired may not be ascertained by the test. To establish if real understanding has taken place it will be necessary to test whether the child can apply such knowledge in order to solve a problem. Both tests are acceptable but it should be absolutely clear to the teacher what is being tested. Knowledge of facts and concept acquisition are not the same thing.

Different types of tests are available to the teacher and these may be internally or externally devised. Criterion assessment is where the criterion is set by the teacher based on his/her own expectation of a child's level of achievement and development. This criterion assessment can be either attainment or ability tests and can be written or verbal. The teacher may pose questions to ascertain whether facts have been learned or whether understanding has been acquired.

Norm-referenced tests on the other hand, test the child to compare him/her with a standard. Some LEAs devise standardized tests for all their schools. A head teacher might devise a standardized test to compare one year group with another. Such testing may or may not test what a child has actually acquired and it will certainly not diagnose areas of difficulty. Diganostic testing does pin point problems the child may be experiencing and teachers can then devise a plan of action to remedy these difficulties.

It is probably the testing of real understanding that is most crucial to the teacher. The Mathematics Inspectorate at the ILEA suggests that within schools an agreed list of concepts, areas of knowledge and skills should be drawn up against which the teacher may ascertain what the child knows and what he understands. This kind of knowledge is of great importance within a school and sometimes it is useful for external agents.

The recipient of the results of the assessment may also influence the nature of the testing and the recording of the results. A future employer will not require the same information as the LEA, the educational psychologist, the parent, the head teacher, the receiving teacher, the receiving school or the pupil him/herself.

It is important not to assess only those parts of the curriculum which are easy to assess, and assessment techniques and tests should not serve to narrow the aims, objectives and approaches required for a mathematics curriculum which is, in the light of the Cockcroft Report[2], broad, balanced and relevant.

It is important to remember that assessment should develop out of the curriculum — its aims, objectives, criteria for content and approaches and not the reverse. Assessment, in whatever form, should never be an end in itself, but a means to an end. The end is the achievement by all pupils of mathematical competence appropriate to their individual abilities and needs, and the development of positive attitudes towards the subject.

It is through the aims and objectives of a sound mathematical curriculum that this end is to be achieved and assessment should be geared to measuring and recording the pupils' progress in relation to these aims and objectives.

Falling Standards

It has to be said that while there is evidence that assessment of children is a positive step towards improving the educational standards in schools, there are dangers which must be considered and avoided. Over recent years the call for a return to the basics has been very loud in some areas. This message has sprung up from varying sources such as the Black Papers in the 1960s, parents, employers and even teachers. A fall in 'standards' was the underlying criticism. It is necessary, however, to look closely at what is meant by standards. There are many differing interpretations which fall into two main areas. Choat maintains that 'standards are specifications by which required qualities may be checked while qualities are degrees of excellence'[3]. The form of mathematical education in which children are encouraged and helped towards concept acquisition and the meaningful application of the concepts is what Choat had in mind and he maintains that the majority of the people who condemn present day standards are not referring to the same criteria at all. Rather, what they refer to is 'basic skills' which are simply a knowledge of the four rules so that children can produce evidence of learning simply by computing page after page of sums. Given enough practice in basic skills children can hardly fail to develop proficiency in this area. But proficiency in basic skills can, and often does, mask a lack of understanding.

Mathematics occurs in everyday situations and if children are to be helped towards recognizing this and being able to deal with it they must have opportunities in school through the mathematics curriculum whereby real understanding and application are an integral part of their mathematics work. Mathematics is inherent in the environment; it has practical uses in everyday life; it is a form of communication with others. Without a full and rich mathematical experience children would not be able to develop as balanced and communicative individuals.

Cockcroft examined this question of the 'basics' and found that whatever term was actually used; and these included such as 'basic skills', 'basic computational skills', 'basic mathematics', 'basic numeracy', the underlying meaning was that the basics were purely arithmetical skills with stress on the four rules of addition, subtraction, multiplication and division, treated in isolation without application to real situations. If mathematics is needed to cope with everyday life then basic skills on their own would seem to be of very limited use. They are simply tools for use in many other areas of mathematics.

Cockcroft concludes 'an excessive concentration on the purely mechanical skills of arithmetic for their own sake will not assist the development of understanding in other areas. It follows that the results of a "back to basics" approach (as we understand these words) are most unlikely to be those which its proponents wish to see, and we can in no way support or recommend an approach of this kind'[4]. So testing in schools should not set out to either refute on the one hand, or fuel on the other, the case of falling standards. Assessment must take account of what qualities the school as part of society wishes its children to possess. Assessment then, will look at degrees of excellence where a school wishes its children to be thinking, balanced, responsible individuals.

Criteria on Assessment and Evaluation

In considering assessment we are looking closely at pupil performance. Not that this is a simple matter — far from it. Within education there are differing opinions on this. Do we assess attainment or achievement? There is a definite difference. Attainment is concerned with the actual performance, whilst achievement is taken as including both performance and how it is achieved. There is a close relationship here with Skemp's viewpoint when he considers understanding. He categorizes two forms of understanding — instrumental understanding and relational understanding. Instrumental understanding is when pupils and teachers think something is understood if they are able to obtain correct answers to a given category of questions without knowing why the method works. This kind of understanding does not necessarily adapt to new requirements and memorising a large number of unrelated rules eventually becomes an impossible burden. Relational understanding though, is not only knowing what to do, but why it is done. This kind of understanding includes knowledge of underlying mathematical relationships and properties. It is more adaptable and is less dependent on outside factors.

In classroom work these two forms of understanding give way to an earlier category which is that of experience. Has the child had experience of certain concepts? This is the necessary fore-runner of any kind of understanding. All these areas require assessment and the assessments will differ according to what is being assessed.

Teachers often experience difficulty in differentiating between these forms of understanding but in reality the progression is not a complicated one. Experience should lead to instrumental understanding which in turn should lead to relational understanding. Some children (and teachers) never progress beyond instrumental understanding whilst other more fortunate individuals can proceed easily from experience to complete relational understanding. Each stage will require different forms of teaching and assessment. The child's position within this progression will determine what the assessment will be examining. Methods used; processes included; determination; use of logic and overall attitudes can all be issues to be considered.

In the document *Mathematics 5–11: A Handbook of Suggestions*[5] four reasons are given for assessment.[5]

(i) for grading;
(ii) to stimulate competition and motivate;
(iii) for diagnostic and guidance purposes;
(iv) to evaluate procedures whereby teaching can be modified.

Whatever the reason is for assessment, it must be used to help the pupils by improving their personal performance and improving the quality of learning that takes place in mathematics. Therefore careful thought must be given to each of these categories.

Grading is commonly used by both LEAs and within schools themselves, but the question arises, what do we learn from grading. What benefits arise from knowing who is top and who is bottom? Are children told where they have made mistakes? or are they simply told of their position or grade?

There may be some children who excel when completing tests and are obviously stimulated by the competition this provides. Many other pupils though feel quite differently. They will become anxious and experience feelings which will turn them off the subject of mathematics. The question of motivation is a difficult one. There seems to be an implication that work itself is not motivating and so we need testing to motivate pupils. Is this to say that schools set up boring tasks for children to do and then find that the only way to motivate them to do this work is to set a test. Testing should be more positive than this.

Diagnosis, on the other hand, seems to take a path which will lead to direct help for the pupil. It can take place in a variety of ways. The teacher can learn of difficulties by day to day contact with the child. Similarly, written work can reveal difficulties but the exact nature of the problem may remain hidden unless the teacher is beside the child at the time of writing. Discussion with the child at the time the difficulties arise is a valuable form of diagnosis and can reveal the exact nature of the child's problems. Formal testing for strengths and weaknesses may sometimes be limited to giving a score or a mathematical age without revealing the nature of the child's learning problem.

Having diagnosed a learning problem it is the job of the teacher to prescribe a suitable programme of work for the child. The teacher must be aware of the resources available to assist in preparing the programme and then he/she must implement it in the way best suited to the child. After what he/she considers to be a reasonable time the teacher must assess again to see if the difficulty has been resolved. This is, in fact, evaluation rather than assessment in that it may be the teaching that has to be modified.

This seems to suggest the following stages in planning a programme of work (see Figure 1).

The many forms assessment can take can be divided into two main categories. They can be informal or formal. Informal assessment can be an integral part of the teacher's daily work. It will take

Assessment and Evaluation

Figure 1: Planning a programme of work

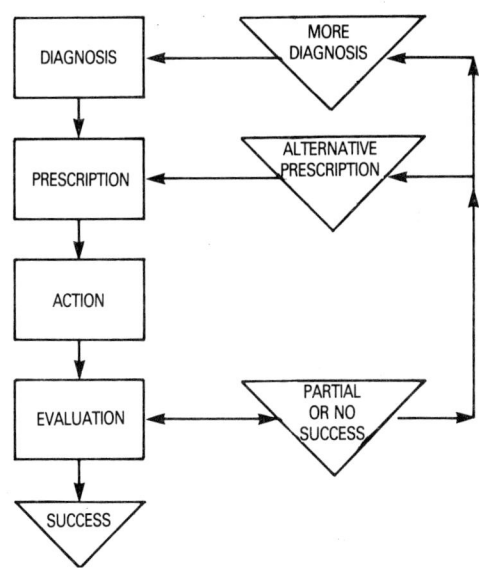

Source: Lumb, D and MM (1986) *Early Mathematics Diagnostic Kit*, Windsor, NFER Publishing Co.

place frequently and be of short duration. Observation; question and answer techniques; and the marking of pupil's work will all fall into this category. Formal assessment, though, will usually entail a planned 'test' and will take place rather less frequently. A deliberate attempt will be made to measure a pupil's progress by the use of either standardized tests, criterion referenced tests or diagnostic tests. These types of tests differ quite markedly in what they assess.

Standardized tests will compare a child with a previously set 'norm' for his age group. The norm will be set to show what is considered a child should know by a certain age. Such tests are usually written tests of the question and answer type. They may measure attainment but not achievement. Obviously some tests will be better than others in this respect.

The shortcomings of standardized test may be overcome by applying a criterion referenced test whereby any particular criteria which the teacher may wish to examine can be scrutinized more closely. In this area of testing great care has to be taken to ensure that it is not simply facts and skills which are tested. The tests should seek to reveal a child's mathematical knowledge in context rather than as artificially separated concepts. The emphasis should be on measuring achievement if the teacher is to acquire a true and accurate judgment of the child. If the teacher only tests facts and skills she will be assessing attainment not achievement. Also there can be a risk in criterion referenced testing for the teacher to teach towards the criteria and the danger is that success in the test may be only temporary. Only when tests are so devised as to take account of the whole range of agreed objectives within the school's curriculum will such dangers be avoided. Certainly well devised criterion referenced testing can reveal illuminating information on achievement which is of the utmost value to the teacher.

There are numerous tests and check lists available to teachers. These can range from simple lists devised by LEAs to very elaborate individualized tests. Some commercially produced tests are so designed as to replace testing by drawing up a pupil profile from a project built on individual discovery. These have suggestions of activities for the child, as well as pointers for the teacher, who observes the child whilst he/she is engaged in the work so that the level of understanding which the child displays can be monitored. Judgment is based on a thorough understanding of mathematical development. Such profiles, properly carried out, will give valuable information about the child. The implementation of such time consuming assessment will be considered later.

Marking

A form of assessment which has an immediate feedback for the child is marking of written work. Positive marking will include comments or other indications to show the child where mistakes have been made. In addition, encouraging or congratulatory remarks on a piece of work will serve to motivate and sustain a child's interest in his work. Discussion of the points raised will further serve to raise the value of marking. It is almost meaningless only to give a mark at the end of the work and it is of very little use to simply put a cross against an incorrect answer. The pupil is not helped at all by this kind of marking and indeed may only be discouraged or frustrated by such actions. Good marking will be diagnostic and supportive. The teacher is also given indication on what should next be taught. Marking and discussion bring to light difficulties either of individuals or whole classes. Marking by the children themselves is often necessary as the teacher cannot possibly mark every piece of work herself. This can be just as valuable so long as the teacher plays an active role. She must ascertain that the marking is accurate

Assessment and Evaluation

and she must keep watch to identify areas of difficulty. The children must have opportunities for discussion if mistakes are to be corrected.

Marking is a very important issue and schools should seek to devise a policy on methods to be used and the purposes of marking. This should be part of the general mathematics policy of the school. *Possible* criteria for marking could include the following:

1. Keep it brief and simple.
2. Make it encouraging.
3. Mark with the child present whenever possible.
4. Discuss marking with the child if he/she is not present at the time of marking.
5. Work for display should be corrected and a fair copy made.
6. Mathematics practice and consolidation work should be marked.
7. Marking must take account of the child's ability to comprehend the error.
8. Credit should be given for correct strategies even though error has made the final solution incorrect.

Record Keeping

Record keeping, once assessments have been made, is an essential element of any school and it is the head teacher's ultimate responsibility to ensure that adequate records are kept. The kinds of records and the type of information to be recorded should be decided by staff discussions. The policies adopted will usually arise from discussion of mathematics already entered into with regard to assessment and evaluation. Records will show progress or otherwise. Lack of progress will not usually be discovered only from records but they are another tool at the disposal of teachers. As with assessment, records can give information on the experiences the child has had as well as the results of tests. The standard record cards which many LEAs require to be completed are often only sufficient to give the briefest information. Schools may have to design their more extensive records if such qualities as a pupil's ability to apply his knowledge when working on problems; or his persistence and confidence in tackling mathematics are to be recorded. The records may show attainment and achievement, or alternatively, they may be a record of topics covered. The school may draw up a record to supplement the LEA's requirements or they may draw up their own record which matches their mathematics scheme (see sample opposite). This kind of record is more likely to make provision for the kind of information which can only be assessed by the professional expertise and judgment of the teacher. For instance, the ability to discuss practical and written mathematics in a coherent manner is a valuable skill which is obvious to the professional observer but may never be apparent in written assessments. Record keeping is admittedly an essential part of education but a correct and sensible balance must be struck otherwise the burden on teachers will be too great. In such situations teachers may have to sacrifice valuable teaching time to administration or they may decide to ignore the keeping of records, to a greater or lesser degree. Neither of these situations is desirable and certainly the teacher's main task is to teach.

Whilst the results of assessment are used directly for record keeping perhaps more importantly they form the basis on which evaluations are made. The teacher can use the results of tests or observations to evaluate the progress of the class and measure these against the aims and objectives set out in the school's scheme of work. Evaluation of this kind gives the teacher opportunities to appraise his/her own teaching. Further, staffs working together can evaluate the content of the scheme; the organization and methods; all forms of apparatus available and the strengths, weaknesses and personal attitudes of the staff. Thus, it will be possible to identify successful practice as well as weaknesses or deficiencies. Only then will it be possible to properly modify policies to ensure that improvements will come about either in individual classes or the school as a whole.

The Assessment of Performance Unit (APU)

Many references have already been made with regard to assessment in that it should cover the whole of the mathematics activity in the classroom. Included will be processes employed by pupils, their attitudes towards mathematics and the application of skills. Over recent years the APU have set out to provide information about general levels of performance and how these alter over a period of time. The terms of reference of the APU are:

> To promote the development of assessing and monitoring the achievement of children at school, and to seek to identify the incidence of under-achievement.[6]

Assessment and Evaluation

This is an example of a mathematics record sheet, but it must be stressed that it is hypothetical. It is not allied to any particular school's mathematics curriculum.

MATHEMATICS RECORD SHEET Practical Work	Name: Computation, etc.							
Number names from 1 to 10		No.	Mon	Lth	Wt.	Vol. Cap	Tme	Dec	F
Recognition of Numbers								
1, 2, 3, 4, 5, 6, 7, 8, 9, 10, 0	+ Unc							
Conservation of Numbers	+ Uc							
Ordering of Numbers	+ T.Unc							
One-to-one Correspondence	+ T.Uc							
Importance of 10	+ HTU.nc							
Recognition of Numbers 11, 12, 13, 14, 15, 16, 17, 18, 19, 20	+ HTU.c							
Conservation of Numbers	+ 4 figs							
Money recognition of coins	+ 5 figs							
Operation of +	+ 7 figs							
Operation of −	− U							
Length — Language	− TU nd							
Shape — recognition of 2D, 3D	− TU d							
Place Value (Base 10)	− HTU nd							
Number sequence to 100	− HTU d							
Counting on and back to 100	− 4 figs							
Composition of Numbers to 100	− 5 figs							
Length — sequence meaning	− 7 figs							
Weight — language	× 2, 4							
Area — Language	× 5, 10							
Counting by grouping (patterns)	× 3, 6							
Division by sharing	× 7, 8, 9							
Time — ¼ past and ¼ to	÷ 2, 4							
Money — shopping and change	÷ 5, 10							
Length — standard unit	÷ 3, 6							
Weight — sequence, meaning	÷ 7, 8, 9							
Area — sequence, meaning	× mult 10							
Vol/Cap. — language	÷ mult 10							
Shape — property of solids	Long ×							
Block graphs	Long ÷							
Place Value (Base 10)	Problems +							
Number sequence beyond 100	Problems −							
Counting on and back	Problems ×							
Place Value (other bases)	Problems ÷							
Fractions — ½, ¾, ⅛, ⅓, ⅙, ⅕, ⅒	Please add further comments on the back of this sheet.							
Weight — standard unit								
Vol/Cap — sequence, meaning								
Shape — right angle								
Time — telling time								
Area — sequence, meaning								
Shape — making solids from nets								
Volume — standard unit								
Bar graphs — scale								
Area — standard unit								
Shape — bilateral symmetry								
Fractions — equivalent fractions								
Length — use of ruler								
Weight — use of weighing machines								
Area of △ and other shapes								
Capacity — standard unit								
Time — a.m./p.m.								
Time — calendar/timetables								
Pie graphs								
Place value — extension to decimals								
Shape — with four sides								
Angles — through rotation								
Grids — fixing position								
Co-ordinates, line graph								
Volume — volume of cuboids								
Averages								
Angle as a means to recognise shape								
Shape — recognition of plane shape								
Fraction, decimal, perc. relationships								

Results of their findings are to be found in the following reports:

Department of Education and Science (1980) *Mathematical Development Primary Survey No. 1*, London, HMSO
Department of Education and Science (1981) *Mathematical Development Primary Survey No. 2*, London, HMSO
Department of Education and Science (1982) *Mathematical Development Primary Survey No. 3*, London, HMSO

The surveys carried out in 1978, 1979 and 1980 involved a random sample of 11-year-olds in England, Wales and Northern Ireland. The APU was concerned to assess the whole range of school education and in order to obtain as broad a picture as was feasible, performances in different kinds of assessment were monitored. There were both written and practical tests. Concepts and skills; problem solving; investigations and attitudes were all examined.

Teachers will be largely interested in assessment materials and the implications to be drawn from the results. The interest will stem from the assessments as methods of testing and also as the source of ideas for curriculum development. Some of the APU's practical tests were concerned with the everyday application of mathematics such as planning a journey. The problem solving element inherent in the tests is very much at the heart of current educational debate in mathematics. Teachers evaluating their curriculum will be paying attention to the success rate of individual questions and the commonly occurring errors with all that they imply for classroom practice.

At present the mathematics section of the APU is in the process of discussing and developing important issues raised by the three surveys. Two further reports are to be issued which will be of interest to primary teachers. One is a full research report on all the surveys so far completed and the second report from a group based at the Cambridge Institute of Education will make recommendations for the classroom. The next survey will be in 1987.

The APU in their wide ranging surveys, have followed a similar progression to that used by teachers in the classroom; that is assessment — discussion of difficulties raised — modification to remedy shortcomings — reassessment after a period of time.

Assessment is an important element in teaching. Used sensibly its implications for improved teaching, both with regard to content

Assessment and Evaluation

and method, are great. However, although assessment is important it should not in any way be allowed to come before teaching in the hierarchy of what is of value in education. Teaching and learning are paramount and nothing should be allowed to alter this fact.

Implementing Assessment and Evaluation Within the School

One of the main themes of this chapter has been the close link between teaching and assessment, the main point being that assessments of all types should arise from the agreed aims and objectives of the school. When considering the mode(s) of assessment(s) to be used within the school there must be a consensus of opinion among the staff if the procedures are to be workable. It is probably wise also to consider making the forms of assessment sufficiently adaptable so that new practices can be incorporated as they arise.

It is not possible or desirable to devise a model for schools to follow. Each school has its own identity known best to its own staff; therefore each school's assessments will differ from those of other schools. There are, however, some general issues which will apply to most, if not all schools, to a certain degree. It is probable that in most primary schools an early diagnostic test would be of value. If difficulties exist in the perception of colour, shape, size and space it is imperative that these are identified as early as possible. Lumb's *Early Mathematics Diagnostic Test* produced by NFER/Nelson in 1986 is one such test available to schools. The test items are divided into the following major areas: colour, shape, size, space, counting, conservation of number, matching, classification, addition, subtraction, multiplication, division, fractions, time, representation language. Each item on the test is a separate card so that concepts are always tested individually.

There is, therefore, no possibility of confusion as to what the child does or does not understand. In addition there is a teacher's manual with the test pack. This is divided into three sections. The first section deals with the background to the test; the second outlines how the test should be administered; and the third section prescribes activities based on the child's responses to the test. A separate sheet for each child is completed by the teacher who is with the child during the test. Relevant information about the responses to the test items are recorded as well as any other informations considered to be relevant or necessary.

Other tests are available and the Mathematical Association has produced a booklet[7] to help teachers in making a suitable choice of tests.

With regard to evaluation, the following booklets published respectively by the Schools Council and the Mathematics Association seek to give guidance:–

(1) *Critical Appraisal Document* (1979)
(2) *Choosing a Primary School Mathematics Textbook or Scheme* (1985)

Both these publications pose relevant questions such that staffs will be guided towards decisions which will be particularly relevant to their organization of the teaching within their school. No definite answers to the questions are given — the final decisions quite rightly being left to the school itself. Some summaries are given but these do not seek to impose any strategies on the readers.

Some of the tests used by the APU can be used by teachers as a basis for developing their own techniques in this field. If a school wishes to engage in practical assessment the APU has developed tests, described earlier in this chapter. Problem solving is at the heart of these tests with the teacher observing pupil responses, noting both success and failure as well as strategies employed. Some of the tests could be adapted to assess the application of skills to everyday situations.

Many schools will devise their own checking system and the ILEA 'checkpoints' can be helpful here. Schools producing checklists may include within the list, some of the personal qualities they wish their pupils to possess. The lists may include such items as:

Is the child able to work independently and logically?
Is the child able to work systematically?
Is the child able to work in a group, cooperatively with others?
Is the child able to discuss and present work appropriately?
Is the child able to show perseverance?

After making their checklist the school will probably record information on individuals as and when appropriate.

All the assessments discussed here are time consuming, especially at the beinning, but it is more than likely that as teachers become familiar with the content and the application of the tests their tasks will become easier. It is likely that teachers will become more astute as observers as a direct consequence of applying assessment which they themselves have helped to form by staff discussions.

Indeed perceptive observation can become part of the teacher's individual teaching approach.

Notes and References

1 DEPARTMENT OF EDUCATION AND SCIENCE (1979) *Mathematics 5–11: A Handbook of Suggestions*, London, HMSO.
2 COCKCROFT, WH (1982) *Report of the Committee of Enquiry into the Teaching of Mathematics in Schools: Mathematics Counts*, London, HMSO.
3 CHOAT, E (1978) *Children's Acquisition of Mathematics*, Windsor, NFER Publishing Co.
4 COCKCROFT, WH (1982) *op cit.*
5 DEPARTMENT OF EDUCATION AND SCIENCE (1979) *op cit*, para 278.
6 DEPARTMENT OF EDUCATION AND SCIENCE (1900) *Mathematical Development Primary Survey No 1*, page XI.
7 MATHEMATICAL ASSOCIATION (1980) *Tests*, Leicester, Mathematical Association.

Notes on Contributors

Chris Bailey is the headteacher of a primary school in the London Borough of Enfield.

Janet Duffin was until recently based in the Department of Educational Studies at the University of Hull, and now is an evaluator with the PRIME Project.

Jeffrey Goodwin is currently a member of the PRIME Project and has recently held posts in a teachers centre and in teacher training.

Brian Hughes is a principal lecturer in mathematics at Rolle College of Higher Education, Exmouth.

David Owen is adviser for primary mathematics with the Devon Education Authority.

Toni McPherson is a lecturer at Rolle College of Higher Education, having recently left a post of mathematics advisory teacher in Dorset.

Gillian Payne is coordinator of the early years course at Rolle College of Higher Education and is widely experienced in nursery and infant work.

Michael Preston is Principal of Rolle College of Higher Education, Exmouth.

Richard Strong is a county adviser for mathematics with the Somerset Education Authority.

Notes on Contributors

Alan Sutcliffe is a senior lecturer in mathematics education at Charlotte Mason College of Higher Education.

Peter Whitfield is a senior lecturer in mathematics education at Newcastle Polytechnic.

Index

Page numbers followed by 'n' refer to notes.

accuracy, levels of 111–12
achievement 157, 159–60
addition, repeated 106
advisers 90–1, 135–50
  action initiated by 146
  curriculum framework 139–41, 142–4, 149
  flexibility 139
  see also coordinators, support services
aims 3–4
algorithms 79–80
approximation 29, 110
  in cooking 57
  measurement 67
  see also estimation
Ashlock, RB 93–4, 103n
assessment 4, 35, 151–67
  APU 143, 162, 164–5
  attitudes and 151–2
  criteria 156–60
  definition 151
  early primary years 80–1
  falling standards 155–6
  implementation 165–7
  marking 160–1
  reasons for 157–8
  record keeping 161–2, 163
  teaching and 152–4
    effectiveness 153
  tests 81, 154, 159–60
  types of 154–5
  see also evaluation
Assessment of Performance Unit 143, 162, 164–5
assignment cards 7, 78–9
Association of Teachers of Mathematics 58, 71n, 92, 128
attainment 157, 159–60
audio visual materials 127–8
Avon Local Education Authority 22, 41n

Bad Tempered Ladybird, The 127, 134n
Bailey, Christine 89–104
  early primary years 80–1
BASIC 119
basics 19–21, 155–6
  see also core curriculum
Bausor, J 71n
BBC programmes 128
bearings 59, 62
Biggs, Mrs 21
Blake, GF 71n
Blythe, K 114, 121n
Bolt, B 22, 41n
'borrowing' 42
Brissenden, TF 45–6, 48, 54n, 55n
British Orienteering Foundation 59, 71n
Bullock report 43, 54n

171

Index

calculators 31–2, 96–7, 105–13, 128–9
  alterations to curriculum 110–13
  existing curriculum 108–11
Calculators and the Mathematics Curriculum 109, 120n
Calculators in the Primary School 32, 41n
capacity measurement 57, 99–100
Carle, E 134n
cassette players 128
central control 72–3
checking 110–11
Child Education 127, 128
Children's Minds 48, 55n
Choat, E 155, 167n
Choosing a Primary School Mathematics Textbook or Scheme 126, 166
Cockcroft report 1, 2, 7, 15n, 16n, 19, 20, 34, 41n, 43, 54n, 73, 88n, 89, 94, 100, 102, 103n, 104n, 105, 113, 116, 120n, 121n, 141, 143, 156, 167n
Collis, Margaret 67, 71n
commercial schemes 91–2, 126–7, 140
communication skills 69
compass bearings 59, 62
computers *see* microcomputers
conceptual structure 58
confidence
  early primary years 77–9, 80
  gender differences 38
  'having a go' 36
  teacher 5, 140
cooking 57
cooperation between schools 83–4
cooperative working 39, 77, 78
coordinators 83–4, 94–5, 137, 138
  see also advisers, support services
core curriculum 2, 10, 72–4
Critical Appraisal Document 166
curriculum
  basics 19–21, 155–6
  content variation 5
  core 2, 10, 72–4
  framework for good practice 139–41, 142–4
  implementation 13, 14, 15
  mathematical education to whole 12
  model 11, 12, 142–3
  planning 1–16, 139
    process 11–13
    responsibility 13, 15
    staged model 11, 12
  seven year cycle 11
  texts, differences between 7
  two parts 9–10, 13

debugging 117–18
decimal fractions 109
decimals, recurring 112
Desforges, C 73, 88n
Developing Mathematical Thinking 131
Dickson, L 106, 120n
Dienes apparatus 126
digital watches 101, 128–9
discussion 7, 21, 34–41, 102–11
  microcomputers and 114–15
  see also language
Donaldson, Margaret 48, 55n
Duffin, Janet 42–55

Early Mathematical Experiences 56, 71n
Early Mathematics Diagnostic Test 159, 165
early years 72–88
  assessment of pupils 80–1
  importance of 75–6
  inservice training 84
  organization 84–6
  pre-school 75–6
  starting school 76–7
Education 5–9 (DES) 76, 88n
Education Observed (DES) 74, 88n
equipment *see* resources
Error Patterns in Computation 93–4, 103n
errors *see* mistakes
estimation 29
  in cooking 57
  measuring 67, 101

Index

see also approximation
Euclid 17
evaluation 4, 35, 46
   definition 151
   see also assessment
Evans, Zoe 47, 55n
expectations 2–3
   parental 74–5
   teacher 80
exposition 7, 21, 22–8, 115

farm visit 68
Flowers of Crystal 115, 121n
Floyd, A 134n
forces 69
Four Cubes 91

gears 70
gender differences 38
   microcomputer use 119
good practice framework 139–41, 142–4, 149
Goodwin, Jeffrey 122–34
grading 158
graphical representation 69, 118
group work 130–3

Hardy, GH 17, 41n
Hart, KM 71n
Haylock, DW 71n
HM Inspectors 1, 15n
   calculators and 105–6, 111
Hounslow Mathematics Centre 97
Hughes, Brian 105–21
Hughes, Martin 43, 54n, 73, 87n

ILEA, Mathematics Inspectorate 154
imperial units 33, 100
individual assignments 7, 78–9
infant classes, topics 57–8
information flow 149–50
in service training 13, 84, 145
INSET 95, 97, 98
instrumental understanding 157
interpretation of data 69
investigatory work 8, 10, 21, 22–8
   calculator use in 112–13

early years 82
software packages 115

Jeffrey, B 103n
Junior Education 127, 128
junior years 89–104

Ladbroke Centre 91
language 2, 42–55, 102, 114
   development 43–4
      in mathematics teaching 44–6
   different meanings 49
   in practice 47–54
   teacher vocabulary 49
   three-term sequence 46
   word recognition 44
   see also discussion
learning
   by rote 79–80
   talk, importance of 43
limit concept 112, 117
Livingstone, J 107, 120n
Logiblocs 126, 129
Logo 98–9, 113, 116–19, 129
Lumb, D and MM 159, 165

McAnulty, Virginia 40
McIntosh, A 40–1
NcNeill, C 71n
McPherson, PT 72–88
Mark, J 92, 103n
marking 160–1
matching (work to need) 31
Mathematical Activities (Bolt) 22, 41n
Mathematical Association 4, 5, 12, 16n, 92, 113, 121n, 126, 134n, 165, 166
   Primary Language Group 46
Mathematical Development Primary Surveys 164
Mathematics across the curriculum 28, 41n
mathematics coordinators *see* coordinators
Mathematics Counts 74, 78, 88n
Mathematics from 5 to 11 19, 34, 41n, 89, 90, 103n, 141, 157
Mathematics from 5 to 16 1, 2, 9,

173

Index

15n, 19, 23, 27, 32, 33, 34, 40, 41n, 56, 71n, 72, 73, 75, 78, 81, 84, 87n, 89, 103n, 107, 112, 141
Mathematics in the Primary School 1, 15n
Mathematics Teaching 40–1
Maths Extra (Avon LEA) 22, 41n
Maths Links 92, 103n
Mation Software 121n
Matthews, Julia 57, 71n
measurement 33–4, 99–101
  accuracy levels 111–12
  in cooking 57
  science experiments 67
  see also capacity
mental arithmetic 92–3, 102, 106
methodology 5, 7–8
  individual assignments 7, 78–9
metric system 33, 100
microcomputers 98–9, 113–20, 128–9
  alterations to curriculum 116–17
  gender differences 119
  in existing curriculum 114–16
Microcomputers in Primary Schools 98, 104n
Microelectronics Education Programme 99, 113
Micro-Primer packs 113
Milner, W 118, 121n
Mindstones-Children, Computers and Powerful Ideas 113
mistakes 93–4
  debugging 117–18
  error patterns 93–4
Mitchell-Potworoski, C 103n
MMI survey 143
modelling 32
motivation 158
Mottershead, L 22, 41n
multicultures 101–2
My Cat Likes to Hide in Boxes 127, 134n

Nash, R 88n
National Association for Remedial Education 92
Newman, C 93, 103n

new technology 128–9
  see also calculators, microcomputers
Newton, WP 71n
Nickels, W 107, 120n
Nuffield Mathematics Project 21
number patterns 96, 112
nursery classes 56–7

objectives 144
Open University 28, 41n, 48, 55n, 70, 71n, 97, 106, 109, 120n, 131, 134n
organization
  early primary years 84–6
  flexible day 85–6
orienteering 59–62, 63
Owen, David 17–41

Papert, Seymour 113, 116–17, 121n
parents
  expectations 74–5
  partners in early years 86–7
patterns
  errors, of 93–4
  number 96, 112
Payne, GM 72–88
Peasey, D 118, 121n
place value 109
plant studies 69
Platt, J 71n
Plunkett, S 93, 103n, 106, 120n
practical work 2, 7, 8, 21, 90
pre-school 75–6
Preston, Michael 1–16
Primary Education in England — A Survey by HM Inspectors of Schools 1, 15n
Primary Practice (School Council) 75, 80, 88n
problem solving 8, 21, 28–34
  calculator use in 112–13
  early primary 77, 82, 85
  software packages 115
proof 39, 40
proportion concept 70
publications 89–90, 127

174

Index

real life situations 58–9, 67–70
   calculators and 111
Recorde, Robert 17, 141n
recording data 69
record keeping 80, 161–2, 163
recurring decimals 112
relational understanding 157
Renfrew, T 71n
repeated addition 106
resource centre 148
resources 122–34
   audiovisual materials 127–8
   buying equipment 124–5
   commercial schemes 91–2, 126–7
   everyday items 125–6
   group work 130–3
   new technology 128–9
     see also calculators, microcomputers
   organization of 129–30
   people 134
   written materials 126–7
Roskope, MF 120n
rote learning 79–80

scale 62–3
   in maps 59–62
Schools Council 15n, 56, 71n, 75, 88n, 166
Schools Curriculum Development Committee 105
science teaching 9, 10
   farm visit 68
   use of mathematics in 67–70
setting 27
seven-year curriculum cycle 11
seven-year difference 20, 73, 94, 109
shapes
   three dimensional 62–3, 68
   two-dimensional 63–6, 68
sharing ideas 37
Shell Centre for Mathematical Education 97
Shuard, Hilary 101, 104n, 105, 106, 108, 120n, 134n
Skemp, 157
Smith, DS 101, 104n

socialization issues 38
Sources of Mathematical Discovery 22, 41n
standardized tests 81, 154, 159–60
Stanfield-Potworoski, J 103n
Straker, Anita 98, 104n, 114, 115, 121n
Strong, Dick 135–50
structures 69
subtractions 40–1
   'borrowing' 42
support services 145–50
   adviser initiated support 146
   areas where needed 136
   beginner teachers and 136–7
   coordinators, for 138
   good practice framework 139–41, 142–4, 149
   information flow 149–50
   in school support 147–8
   in service courses 13, 84, 145
   mid-career teachers 137–8
   resource centres 148
   staff 148–9
   teacher initiated support 145–6
   teacher 'persuaded' support 146
   working groups 147
   see also advisers, coordinators
surveys 118
Sutcliffe, Alan 56–71
Sutton, E 134n

Taback, 112
teachers
   advisory *see* advisers
   beginners, support for 136–7
   confidence 5, 140
   early primary years 81–3
   'importance pressures' 9, 20
   inservice education 13, 84, 145
   mid-career 137–8
   training 8
   see also coordinators, support services
teaching
   assessment and 152–4
   methods 5, 7–8